Growing Up in Stages

COGNITIVE
DEVELOPMENT
OF THREE- AND
FOUR-YEAR-OLDS

Susan A. Miller, EdD

Gryphon House
www.gryphonhouse.com

Published by Gryphon House, Inc.
P. O. Box 10, Lewisville, NC 27023
800.638.0928; 877.638.7576 (fax)
Visit us on the web at www.gryphonhouse.com.

Bulk Purchase
Gryphon House books are available for special premiums and sales promotions as well as for fund-raising use. Special editions or book excerpts also can be created to specifications. For details, call 800.638.0928.

Disclaimer
Gryphon House, Inc., cannot be held responsible for damage, mishap, or injury incurred during the use of or because of activities in this book. Appropriate and reasonable caution and adult supervision of children involved in activities and corresponding to the age and capability of each child involved are recommended at all times. Do not leave children unattended at any time. Observe safety and caution at all times.

Library of Congress Cataloging-in-Publication Data
The Cataloging-in-Publication Data is registered with the Library of Congress for ISBN 978-0-87659-725-5.

DEDICATION

To Gregg, my brilliant and caring son who was my original inspiration for writing about preschool development so many years ago.

To Peter, my husband and best friend for fifty years. With the greatest appreciation for his always being my champion and serving as the most amazing mentor for students of all ages.

PRAISE FOR SUSAN A. MILLER'S BOOKS IN THE GROWING UP IN STAGES SERIES

SHARON MACDONALD,
author and educator

Susan has been a personal friend and a resource for me since my classroom days teaching four-year-olds in San Antonio, Texas, and on through my years on the road speaking to teachers about the ages and stages of early childhood development. I always sought out her opinions and insights. Now I do not have to call her. I have her books!

Her understanding of social, cognitive, and emotional development in young children is unrivaled. She explains ages and stages in her unique way—clean, simple, honest. She is a gifted writer with real empathy and understanding for her subjects—children.

Susan Miller's books belong in the personal library of any early childhood teacher. Buy them.

DEBBIE VERA
PhD, associate professor and chair of the Department of Educator and Leadership Preparation, Texas A&M University

While reading the scenarios, I could easily see how all three domains in this series—emotional, social, and cognitive development—are interdependent. This series provides a holistic view of the child and really helps the reader to understand the overlap of development into each domain.

The writing style is personal and engaging for teachers.

CONTENTS

ACKNOWLEDGMENTS

My family, Peter, Gregg, Owen, and Adam, for their support and patience.

My typist of many years, Karen Epting, for her professionalism and sense of humor.

Librarian Julie Daigle, for her invaluable assistance with researching children's books.

Diane Ohanesian, for encouraging me to write this series.

Gryphon House staff members Stephanie Roselli, for answering my many questions; Terrey Hatcher, for her thorough and very thoughtful editing; and Anna Wilmoth, for her assistance with details and publicity.

INTRODUCTION

After almost forty years in the field of early childhood education as a teacher, director, college professor, and supervisor of student teachers, I never cease to marvel at the many ways young children use their creativity and critical thinking to solve problems or design something unique. As an educator, I feel it is so very important to tune into children's interests and give them sufficient space and materials, as well as adequate time to experiment and explore.

One of my favorite memories of three- and four-year-olds being challenged as they developed their cognitive skills was at the Kutztown University of Pennsylvania Early Learning Center when a father brought in a gigantic box of hundreds of natural-wood circles about the size of 1-inch-thick poker chips. After we dumped out the box, many of the preschoolers eagerly burrowed through the huge pile of intriguing wooden circles with squeals of delight, while a few others watched in amazement. Some gathered them up in their hands and then let them trickle through their fingers. A few began to stack the circles, while others made long parades or created numerous rows. Each day, wonderful new things occurred. Children tried to count how many circles were in their piles or rows. They made graphs of how high they could build. A group circled the room with a chain of circular chips and then dictated a story about it. Some four-year-olds made the letters in their names by connecting the wooden circles. Groups of builders worked cooperatively as they planned, designed, and engineered flat and three-dimensional forms, such as castles, amusement parks, and more! But the highlight of the circle creations occurred when the fifth-grade reading buddies worked with them to construct an enormous circular beehive. The children sent out invitations so they could share the elaborate structure that the team of three-, four-, and ten-year-olds had built with great enthusiasm. The whole school admired the structure during an informative question-and-answer session.

Each day, the children were engaged with what they called the "circle box." They buried gold-painted discs in sand as pirates' treasure and placed colored discs in plastic bottles, which they turned into festive maracas that they shook with enthusiasm. These natural learning materials helped challenge and expand the preschoolers' cognitive skills in various developmental stages. It was astonishing how such creative pleasure erupted from simple pieces of discarded wood.

What You Will Notice

Young children's cognitive skills develop very quickly during their first few years of life. Their curiosity stimulates their thinking skills and creativity as they rapidly become budding scientists, engineers, artists, readers, and writers. Three- and four-year-olds turn into amazing problem solvers when faced with challenging situations, such as what to do when their wagon becomes mired in the mud.

But, of course, they are not always using their brains for practical matters. Preschoolers' magical thinking can be very powerful when they wish for something to happen, even though it may be illogical. For example, the wished-for snow at bedtime as a child thinks about trying out his new red sled becomes simply magical when he wakes up to find wonderful white snow covering the ground.

You will find that four-year-olds are often noisy and messy, as their curiosity inspires them to jump right in to see what is going on. They love to use tools to investigate while they take things apart to see how they work. On the other hand, three-year-olds may hold back a bit to see what others are doing. If something seems a little scary, they might ask lots of questions and might want the teacher to explore with them. Nevertheless, preschoolers are intrigued when they are challenged with novel situations.

A key challenge for three- and four-year-olds is learning about time. Because time is invisible, it is a confusing and abstract concept for preschoolers. They need to have lots of experience with temporal concepts in personal ways, such as birthdays, bedtime, and story time. Inclined to be egocentric, preschoolers find the time they are in at the moment, the present, most important.

Besides time, preschoolers are also exploring space. Their knowledge of spatial awareness is related to their own bodies. Over time, spatial concepts are enhanced through involvement with concrete experiences and situations with objects and people. For example, constructing with blocks with friends can provide amazing experiences to explore the concept of spatial awareness as preschoolers arrange and rearrange items. These interactions also can help children grasp an understanding of locational prepositions, such as *in*, *under*, *behind*, and *down*.

Faced with daily problems to solve, preschoolers use their imaginations and thinking skills to come up with fascinating solutions. Three-year-olds might use a trial-and-error approach and may center on a single phenomenon. Four-year-olds are busy learning to use a problem-solving approach as they brainstorm solutions and then try out some of the suggestions before selecting a workable idea. The problem-solving process commonly involves their critical-thinking and creative-thinking skills.

For preschoolers, expressing themselves creatively with paint, crayons, colored markers, clay, and collage materials is exciting and a whole lot of fun. As young children experiment with color, shapes, textures, and design, they discover new and different ways to creatively express their feelings. They pass through many fascinating stages on their creative journey, from drawing unrecognizable forms, to creating with intention, to painting things that are more realistic.

Preschoolers are also working to develop their mathematical thinking. This intriguing process is infused throughout the day as preschoolers learn about patterns and notice sequences of shapes, colors, movements, or sounds that repeat themselves. This awareness can help preschoolers see relationships among various aspects of their environment. Ordering and seriating can happen rather spontaneously in the block area as children build tall structures or lay out a city. Many hands-on explorations are related to numbers, as three- and four-year-olds learn about one-to-one correspondence and measurement.

You will see that preschoolers are only too happy to participate in scientific investigations. These might be floating and sinking discoveries or physics experiments with gravity applications as marbles roll down a wooden ramp. Four-year-olds, in particular, love to use a scientific-inquiry approach. They may need to go through many illogical thinking processes before they can even begin to make some sense of concepts. But that's half the fun of it!

As young children explore their capabilities, learning to write can bring them such satisfaction. Handwriting is more than just holding pencil to paper. To develop the pincer grasp, a child might practice threading large beads to strengthen the coordination of the finger muscles and thinking skills. By providing many wonderful examples of print and writing instruments, teachers can create an environment conducive to introducing preschoolers to the writing process. Young children move at their own rates from a controlled-scribbling stage to writing mock letters in word-like strings. Then children revel in an exciting achievement—they can write their own names! This development is followed by more writing with invented or phonetic spellings as they explore writing word groupings. These accomplishments fuel such empowerment for emergent writers.

More than simply learning to decode words, emergent readers should be enveloped by a print-rich environment, where they can be immersed in hands-on involvement with print-related activities and conversations. Reading aloud to young children is an extremely important activity for literacy. Using alphabet, rhyming, and predictable books can be a wonderful springboard to enhance preschoolers' potential to become lifelong readers.

This book is designed to help you understand the range of cognitive abilities of three- and four-year-olds and learn useful strategies for encouraging the growth of preschoolers in your care.

As You Read This Book

As you start each chapter, you will find a definition for the chapter's theme. As you read on, you may wish to think about and add your own definition on a sticky note.

Next are some highlights of developmental milestones of three- and four-year-olds. These will help you understand the stage of cognitive development that a preschooler is functioning in during a specific time.

Then I will share some scenarios related to the chapter topic. These snapshot views are taken from events that happened with the children in my various classrooms (names changed, of course), from observations that I have been fortunate enough to make in preschool programs around the United States and abroad, and from special memories of my grandsons at particular three- and four-year-old stages. Related to the different scenarios are explanations of the stages to help you understand why a behavior or action is or is not occurring at that specific time. As we are all aware, individual preschool children may develop at different rates—some a little slowly, and others more rapidly.

Although I would like very much to have a face-to-face conversation with each reader, that of course is not possible. So what I have tried to do, as the author and a teacher, is to write in a conversational tone discussing the stages that young children go through. Rather than burdening you with heavy research and theoretical references, I have attempted to keep the flow of observation and application light and practical.

Next, you will discover guidance specifically for you, the teacher or caregiver. The section called What You Can Do is designed to serve as a springboard by providing exciting curriculum activities or helpful teaching strategies for you to try with the children in your care. Feel free to build on these ideas and write on sticky notes to make this section your own.

The Other Aspects to Consider—Alerts section deals with circumstances that you might have questions about, such as when young children are not quite in step with the cognitive-development milestones for their age. This may indicate that you or a child's parents should consider seeking professional assistance for answers.

The ideas offered in the Activities for Parents to Try at Home portion are fun, easy-to-accomplish adventures appropriate for parents to explore with their children. You may wish to share these ideas with parents during conferences, online, in your newsletter, or by posting on a bulletin board. If you like, ask parents to share their own ideas on the topic and to provide photos of the activities for everyone to enjoy afterward.

Finally, a special section suggests fascinating books to read with children. All of the literature is related to the chapter topic and just begs you and the children to look at the enticing pictures, talk about the words, and enter into a dialogue about what is happening on the pages. Research shows that reading to young children is the most important way to stimulate their desire to become readers.

As you read this book, I hope you enjoy your adventures observing young children and learning how various cognitive-development milestones affect the different stages of the lives of three- and four-year-olds.

Cognitive Development of Three- and Four-Year-Olds

1

BELIEVING IN
MAGICAL THINKING

Magical thinking—a rather irrational belief that by just wishing for or thinking about something you have the power to cause it to happen

hen you're aware of some of the tendencies toward magical thinking among three- and four-year-olds, you can better support the challenges that might occur as they develop their cognitive skills. Although not all children develop at the same rate or achieve specific milestones at the same time, the following snapshots highlight some of the behaviors you might see as preschoolers' magical thinking evolves:

- Three-year-olds tend to feel responsible if something upsetting happens because they tend to perceive things that occur as relating to themselves.
- Three-year-olds may be influenced by their magical thinking when an adult tries to convince them to do something.
- Because of three-year-olds' lack of experience, certain aspects of their thinking sometimes appears almost magical.

- Four-year-olds frequently take things that others say literally, such as "I'm so tired my feet are going to fall off."
- Four-year-olds often attribute lifelike characteristics to inanimate objects.
- Magical and animistic thinking can easily affect four-year-olds' reasoning.

Now, let's consider some scenarios of how magical thinking might affect the interactions and behaviors of children in your classroom.

At the imaginary sidewalk café, three-and-a-half-year-old Amy and four-year-old Tessa serve tea and honey cakes to their stuffed bears. Ashley, an uninvited guest, keeps trying to join the two best friends' party. She finally picks up a teacup, then attempts to eat some cakes. Very annoyed with Ashley's unwanted actions, the girls tell her, "Get away from our party. Don't ever come back!" When Ashley does not come to school for the next few days, the girls are initially happy she is not interrupting their play. However, they begin to worry that Ashley isn't at school because they told her to leave. They think that maybe they should let their teacher know what they did in case Ashley doesn't show up soon.

Egocentric thinking, or the tendency for preschoolers to perceive things that occur as they relate to themselves rather than from another's point of view, can cause young children like Amy and Tessa to feel responsible when something bad or upsetting happens. Children may decide to use their magical thinking if they really want something to happen, such as making Ashley go away. Then when it occurs, they believe they are the ones who caused it to happen through their actions. When Ashley developed stomach flu and did

not come to school, the girls believed her disappearance was their fault because they were angry that Ashley ruined their party and they wished she would leave.

As preschoolers use their imaginations, they enjoy participating in pretend play. It gives them exciting opportunities to try out various identities and attempt to understand how others think. Magical thinking frequently intersects with imaginative play. This type of play can reinforce preschoolers' amazing beliefs about what they think might or might not happen. Between two and seven years of age, while in Piaget's preoperational stage of cognitive development, preschoolers often become confused about what is real

Cognitive Development of Three- and Four-Year-Olds

and not real. They are not always sure if what they are thinking in their heads is really occurring in the everyday world.

Adults frequently tap into magical thinking to convince young children to try something. For example, a parent might say, "Eat all of your spinach so you will have strong muscles like Popeye!" Along similar lines, the teacher observes Carla holding her sick baby doll in the dramatic play area. Following her mother's modeling, Carla says, "Eat your chicken soup. Then your cold will be all better."

When preschoolers use magical thinking, they can't always objectively determine causes and effects. Their desires often skew their perceptions of events. For example, several four-year-old boys are convinced that the comic-book characters called the Teenage Mutant Ninja Turtles are coming to join them on the playground. They are sure that if they yell down through the holes in the sewer cover each day, they can encourage the characters to climb out of the sewer. Imagine their delight when one morning they notice the cover has been turned over and echoing sounds are coming from the underground sewer. Thrilled, they inform their teacher that the Ninja Turtles must have arrived overnight. Their wish came true! It doesn't matter that there was a huge thunderstorm that created a loud rushing flood of water that required removal of the cover by the town's water system workers.

Preschoolers frequently interpret interactions literally because they lack experience. Bryan looks at his older brother in amazement and backs up a little when his brother says, "My stomach is so full it is going to explode!" When Rita's father shows her teacher his new car, the teacher announces, "I'm turning green with envy." Puzzled, Rita carefully checks out her teacher for signs of a color change.

Preschoolers frequently attribute lifelike characteristics to inanimate objects. Their magical and animistic thinking can easily affect their reasoning. Very excited, three-year-old Charles tells his teacher, "You know, my shadow follows me. It knows how to run and jump, too!" He associates life with forms of movement. Preschoolers frequently illogically attribute the causes of common occurrences.

And, of course, the mystical, magical influence of Santa Claus is a big deal for many preschoolers! The whole tale is quite believable to them as they see a real-looking Santa at the mall and during holiday events. Adults ask children to make lists for Santa or tell Santa what they wish for. When they wake up with presents under the tree, it is not hard for young children to believe that their magical thinking has, indeed, made wishes come true!

As children grow up, their dreams help mold them into who they become. A while ago, a delightful little boy named George spread his pretend wings and flitted freely around my preschool classroom. Each day, he generously shared information about the kind of butterfly he was and described the different colorful patterns on his wings. We fondly called him "butterfly boy." Today, this once-intriguing magical young thinker is a celebrated artist known for his beautifully detailed butterfly paintings!

What You Can Do

- **Note cause and effect.** Ask, "Now what do you think happens?" Or question the child about his view of why things took place the way they did. Try to avoid using leading questions, such as "Are you afraid the dog might bite you?"
- **Provide interesting art supplies.** Offer fingerpaints, colorful markers, and different sizes of paintbrushes for young children to use to artistically depict their magical thinking. Expressing themselves through drawing and painting provides another venue of communication for preschoolers who may be unable to verbalize their magical thoughts.
- **Encourage children to act out situations.** Dramatizing various roles from books, such as *Jack and the Beanstalk*, can help preschoolers feel empowered during pretend scary moments. It is important for young children to have experiences with make-believe and real scenarios to clarify situations and events in their magical thinking.
- **Set out a sensory box.** Include items that will appeal to children's various senses. For sight, you might supply sparkly fabrics and rainbow-colored ribbons. For sound, you might set out giant seashells for holding up to their ears and seeds for shaking in tiny canisters. For smell, you could stock pine needles and herbal tea bags. For touch, you might supply rough pine cones and soft cotton balls. Change the sensory items every few days to trigger new creative thoughts and experiences.
- **Ask children to think about what they would like to be.** During circle time or with a small group of preschoolers, ask each one to make a magical wish and tell what he would like to

be—a unicorn, a farmer, a wizard. Encourage fun descriptions, such as "I want a pointy green horn" or "I need a twirly purple cape." Provide a box of accessories—containing items such as fabric, shoes, hats, feathers, and tape—to help bring their magical wishes to life.

Other Aspects to Consider—Alerts

- **Be aware of your responses.** To be reassuring, explain things in simple, concrete terms. For example, a preschooler may wish to play with the class guinea pig that has recently died. It is confusing and possibly a little frightening if you use abstract concepts to tell the child she is not able to because the class pet has "gone to sleep" or "is resting up in heaven." These comments are difficult for her to understand because to her these physical actions are really about a temporary loss. The magical thinking preschooler might easily believe that the animal will come back when it wakes up if she wishes for that to happen.

- **Be reassuring.** When a preschooler wishes something bad to happen to someone, and then it does, you may need to reassure him that his thinking did not cause the event and he is not responsible. For example, because he does not want to follow his teacher's rules, he tells her, "I want you to go far away to China!" Then she is transferred to another class. When he feels sad and misses her, you may need to comfort the child. You could explain that she is now the toddler teacher because the center has added a new program, but they will always have a special connection because she was his teacher. Help him try to understand that he will not be able to reverse her assignment, even if he wishes very hard.

- **Go with the flow.** Magical thinking is quite normal for preschoolers and will disappear as they grow a little older. For example, young children are showered with advertisements on TV and in stores that use characters in costumes. A clown, a life-size costumed character from a book or TV show in the mall, or a colorful costumed team mascot looks huge to young children. To preschoolers with animistic thoughts, these make-believe characters seem alive with lifelike qualities, and children expect certain actions from the characters. Because preschoolers are egocentric, they are inclined to believe that everyone shares their perspective. Try not to be judgmental. It won't help to argue that the imagined activity won't really happen, so you might just want to join in the fun or at least be a good listener.

Activities for Parents to Try at Home

- **Collect props.** Gather interesting items such as scarves, bags, junk jewelry, and towels. Encourage your child to play freely with these props to enhance her imagination as she becomes interesting characters, such as a princess, a ballerina, a superhero, or a circus performer. Take lots of magical photos. Then enlarge them to display like whimsical posters.

- **Listen to a variety of fun music.** Together, twirl and dance the jitterbug to jazz and exotic beats. Move fast like cheetahs or hop like kangaroos. Turn your living room into a magical ballroom! Maybe you can add an old rotating reflective disco ball from a flea market.

- **Tune into holiday magic.** Make wishes come true! Provide glue, tape, colored paper, scissors, crayons, glitter, and ribbons so your child can design whimsical presents, cards, and decorations for others. For birthdays and holidays, preschoolers like to create lists of gifts they are hoping for.

- **Design a magical wand.** Create this special accessory with your child to turn ordinary things and events into something uniquely magical. Together, make up a funny rhyme, such as "razzle-dazzle-roo," to use with the wand.

- **Create a family wish book.** Draw pictures, cut out magazine images, and take photos with a camera. Glue these in a scrapbook. Share dreams about vacation plans and real or make-believe activities. Infuse your family's storybook with magical thinking—the sky is the limit!!

Related Books to Read with Children

Hoffman, Mary. 1991. *Amazing Grace.* New York: Dial Books for Young Readers.

Joosse, Barbara M. 1991. *Mama, Do You Love Me?* San Francisco: Chronicle Books.

Ringgold, Faith. 1991. *Tar Beach.* New York: Crown.

Williams, Margery. 2014. *The Velveteen Rabbit.* Kennebunkport, ME: Applesauce.

Zolotow, Charlotte. 1972. *William's Doll.* New York: Harper & Row.

2

DEMONSTRATING A
SENSE OF CURIOSITY

Curiosity—being inquisitive to learn about something or somebody

Preschoolers want to know how things work, what happens if they try some new activity, where things come from, and so on. Their curiosity steers them in interesting directions. Although all children develop at different rates, you are likely to see some of the following characteristics among the three- and four-year-olds in your care as their curiosity leads them to explore their world:

- Three-year-olds ask lots of questions of adults to help satisfy their curiosity.
- Three-year-olds often fixate on their curiosity and may focus for as long as ten minutes without being distracted.
- Three-year-olds are curious and maybe a little frightened about scary things, so they may need adult reassurance.
- Four-year-olds enjoy curious surprises and observing changes take place right in front of them.

- Four-year-olds are fascinated by the mysteries of nature and may use special tools (such as a trowel or magnifying glass) to help them investigate.
- Because four-year-olds are curious about how things work, they will take them apart and figure out how to put them back together again.

Now let's consider some anecdotes that illustrate how children in your classroom might follow their curiosity and make new discoveries.

Because of a heavy rainfall, Ms. Beverley's preschoolers could not go out to play in the morning. Now that the sun is shining, they eagerly run out on the playground. Three-year-old Cora points to a huge puddle and asks, "What is that big water?" Ms. Beverley responds, "A puddle." Cora questions, "Where did it come from?" She observes four-year-old Binh throw a small stone into the puddle. Sharing this novel event with his friends, he exclaims, "Look! My stone made rings on the water!" Several others enthusiastically try this, too.

Maggie, a four-year-old, throws in the head of a yellow dandelion. She tells the gathering crowd of preschoolers, "Hey! The flower is floating." Wearing boots, four-year-old Cooper stomps through the puddle while loudly yelling, "Boom! Boom!" Water sprays everywhere as the children giggle.

Everyone knows that if a puddle is nearby, a young child is sure to find it. Why are preschoolers so curious about their surroundings? When they notice changes or that something is different, they automatically become intrigued. However, they may react to this interest in different ways. For instance, when three-year-old Cora noticed something

Cognitive Development of Three- and Four-Year-Olds

strange on the playground, she asked her teacher several questions so she could get answers to satisfy her curiosity. Three-year-olds, like Cora, are also apt to observe others' investigations from a safe distance until they feel comfortable exploring. Four-year-olds, like Binh and Maggie, are more confident and love to jump right in to experiment. They enjoy having others become involved as they share their ideas.

As preschoolers explore the world around them, their senses help to enhance their curiosity. Typical of a four-year-old boy, Cooper makes bold loud noises with his voice and his feet as he stomps in the water to see what will happen. Adventurous, four-year-olds often go over the top with their zestfulness to explore their curiosity, as evidenced by Cooper splashing everyone. Acting on curiosity can frequently be messy! All along, Cooper was making good use of his senses of hearing, sight, and touch to help him investigate his interactions with the water-filled puddle.

Although a change in the environment or a behavior may be one thing that attracts a preschooler to a situation or a particular item and arouses his curiosity, novelty is a surefire way to create interest. For example, four-year-old Luna finds something she had never seen before in a cup in the art area. Six sticks of black charcoal poke out of a container. Curious as to what to do with them, thinking they are sort of like little pencils or maybe black crayons, Luna grabs some paper to see if the charcoal creates marks when she draws. She makes small, skinny, black lines. Then she tries drawing with a stick on its side. Fascinated, she shouts to her friends, "Surprise! Big black clouds. And look at my messy black hands." Curious four-year-olds, like Luna, often find it helpful to clarify their thinking by looking at or considering items' similarities or differences (such as charcoal sticks, pencils, and black crayons) to help them create a meaningful classification (in this case, drawing instruments). Three- and four-year-olds often show a curiosity about open-ended art media (such as chalk and playdough), as evidenced by Luna's delight with how spontaneous she is able to be with the charcoal.

In order to keep preschoolers' interest, it is necessary to find challenging ways to keep their curiosity alive. This is especially important for three-year-olds, who have short attention spans. Knowing this, before her class left the playground Ms. Beverley drew a big line with sidewalk chalk all around the puddle on the dry part of the blacktop. With heightened curiosity, the boys and girls wanted to know what she was doing. To stimulate their interest, she slyly said, "We'll need to investigate tomorrow!" Imagine their surprise when the puddle wasn't near the chalk outline anymore. They wondered, "Did the puddle shrink?" Maggie checked to see if her flower was still floating. Many questions were asked, and enthusiastic suggestions were given to unravel the mysteries!

Have you ever observed a young child who has discovered something special that piques his curiosity? He feels empowered to bring his friends, one or two at a time, to very quietly observe this curious attraction. One afternoon, Mrs. Adams noticed two of the four-year-old boys following Evan on tiptoe to the forsythia bush, where they shared the excitement of secretly peeking at three

tiny eggs in a bird's nest. For a few days, the boys continued to carefully observe the nest until the eggs finally hatched. They created nests of their own out of twigs and dried grass. Captivated by the wonders of nature, four-year-olds are able to look at things from different perspectives. And they love the surprise of watching change occur right before their very eyes.

At times four-year-olds, especially boys, like to live on the edge. They are curious about behaviors as well as items or events. Sometimes their curiosity can be risky. They wonder who can jump the farthest off the jungle gym or ride a tricycle the fastest. This fascination frequently makes them feel rather important, like a big kid or a superhero. And certain things that capture their interest can be downright dangerous, such as sticking a finger in a broken clock to see how the hands move or cracking open raw acorns and then trying to eat them, unaware that the nuts might make them sick.

When big, dark thunder clouds and lightning appeared outside the classroom window, three-year-old Betsy was both fascinated and frightened. While she watched through the window, Betsy heard a loud boom, and the power went off. She ran to Mrs. Molina and hid under her arm. Because three-year-olds are still in the process of determining if something is real or not, they often need reassurance or encouragement to explore a situation that has aroused their curiosity. For example, later when Betsy wonders if the scary thing on the wall is a shadow or a monster, she and Mrs. Molina investigate and experiment with hand shadow puppets together to see what Betsy thinks.

Preschoolers enjoy exhibiting a healthy curiosity about how things work. Three-year-olds, who may focus for as long as ten minutes without becoming disinterested, often fixate on the target of their curiosity. Sebastian watches the gears go around as he turns the handle on the egg beater in the soapy water tub. He stares at the bubbles the whirling blades create. Curious to investigate further what else the egg beater's blades might do, he places them on top of a huge ball of playdough and turns the handle. From the look on Sebastian's face, he is surprised when they get stuck in the dough!

Four-year-olds, however, love to take things apart and put them back together. This no doubt accounts for their fascination with big-piece jigsaw puzzles. Cole and Yoshrar try to connect their wooden block skyscrapers, but the structures keep toppling over. Curious to figure out why, they pull the block structures apart and discuss their strategy as they build again. Cole suggests, "Let's put only big blocks on the bottom." After a few false starts, the boys engage in an engineering process. Solving their problems as they test their solutions, these curious boys finally align the two block skyscrapers so the bridge connects them successfully.

Related to their egocentricity, three-year-olds are keenly curious about themselves and their bodies. My grandson Owen keeps wondering what his leg looks like under the stick-on bandage. Intrigued, he removes the bandage to discover a scab over his spider bite. Still curious and a little squeamish, he picks at the scab until it begins to bleed. His curiosity satisfied, Owen asks for a replacement bandage so the bite won't look so "yucky."

Three-year-old Aubree is sitting next to the class's foster grandmother. Aubree notices that their arms look different, and she has many questions. For example, why is Mrs. Metzgar's skin wobbly and wrinkly? And why is Aubree's own skin smooth?

Able to look more outside of themselves, four-year-olds are quite  curious about what adults are doing and why. When several children notice the piano tuner, they bombard her with questions: "Why are you opening the piano top? Can we look inside? What is that metal thing?" She explains that it is a tuning fork. When she finishes, they want to know, "Will you play the piano? We will sing!" Asking questions like these is a huge help as preschoolers try to make sense of their curiosity.

What You Can Do

- **Create a novelty center.** Gather intriguing collections, such as stones, seashells, magnets, and pinecones. Keep them in see-through boxes for easy identification and access by the children. Place a collection of curiosities on a table for the children to explore for a while. When their interest wanes, put out a new collection to challenge their curiosity. Encourage preschoolers to add their own interesting items to the table to share with others.

- **Add little surprises to other centers.** You can arouse the preschoolers' curiosity to think of new ways to use established areas. For example, at the art easel, add different variations of brushes, such as toothbrushes, baby bottle brushes, pine needles, or feathers. In the block center, hang motivational posters of a castle, skyscraper, bridge, and Stonehenge to suggest new building styles. Add different equipment, such as a whisk, chopsticks, or a Bundt pan, to the home area on a rotational basis to spark interest as the children experiment with the items.

- **Offer the unexpected.** A Ganado, Texas, preschool teacher calls this activity "Sabotage." She provides blindfolds to use with sand play. The curious children try to guess what they are playing with buried in the sand and then share their ideas. Preschoolers start with clear plastic cups of water and add different things, such as dirt, salt, liquid soap, and ice cubes. Then, they stir to stimulate their curiosity about what occurs. After fingerpainting at the art center, a teacher introduces shaving cream, pudding, or mud to the children so they can actively explore and describe their curious new tactile experience.

- **Change stories to build curiosity.** Change the ending or middle of some of the preschoolers' favorite stories. With a different twist, engage their curiosity to create suggestions or new endings. What if Cinderella didn't lose her shoe? Or Goldilocks didn't run away? To create more interest, add a novel character such as a dinosaur to Little Red Riding Hood's escape.

- **Invite a mystery guest.** For a few days before, build up the children's curiosity about their guest's impending visit. Encourage their questions. Your guest might arrive in a uniform (possibly a firefighter, soldier, police officer, or mail carrier) or a costume (maybe a clown or ballet dancer). Ask your mystery visitor to bring along any special equipment, such as a toolbox or a beekeeper's protective gear, to arouse the children's interest. Let the children ask questions and appropriately explore any related materials. Provide resource books with lots of pictures. Use technology to provide an exciting website for the children to extend their interest and continue to find out more about the person's job or life.

Other Aspects to Consider—Alerts

- **Be aware of dangerous situations.** When young children are excited about exploring and experimenting with interesting items, they might place themselves in dangerous situations, such as poking a wiggly snake with a stick. They like to observe adults and enjoy copying adults' actions. For example, after their teacher places the prongs of a plug into the wall outlet, Tracy considers pushing her barrette closure into the outlet to see what will happen. The teacher notices Tracy's focus on the outlet, makes sure it has a safety cover, and explains the danger. Because accidents can easily happen, make sure that children always have proper supervision so that they can explore their curiosity safely.

- **Don't show your distaste for their curiosity.** As children explore novel materials, their curiosity can be very messy! Try to set up the environment so it can be easily cleaned up, rather than discouraging the children's experiences by always telling them, "Don't make a mess. Keep your clothes clean." Preschoolers quickly pick up on an adult's disapproval or disgust concerning a mess, which may curb their future curiosity.

- **Some children appear anxious.** Because of their temperaments, learning styles, or possibly frightening past experiences, certain young children are reluctant to attempt new activities or explore objects. Fearful children may not wish to touch unusual materials, such as shaving cream or wet sand. If that is the case, you can provide tongs or gloves to help them experiment comfortably. Others might be too shy to participate in a novel activity, such as placing a hand in a sensory box. They will need lots of time to observe others' explorations. They will also require patience and reassurance from teachers and parents.

Activities for Parents to Try at Home

- **Create a surprise bag.** Tap into your child's senses. Raise his level of curiosity by urging him to shake the bag and listen, reach in and feel the item, or sniff to guess what it might be. For instance, if it is a cotton ball, he might say, "It feels soft." You could add, "It is white." He might reply, "It feels round. Like a little ball." If he can't guess, allow him to look or reach in. Continue this banter with comments while he explores his exciting discovery. Encourage him to find a curious item for the surprise bag for you to investigate.

■ **Design an investigation box.** Young children love to explore outdoors. They will find an endless supply of items to discover when they are immersed in the natural world. To make their investigations twice as much fun, prepare tools to support their explorations. Create a box with a shovel, trowel, sifter, butterfly net, plastic jar with a lid, plastic magnifier, small paper bags, and so on. When your curious young explorer wants to dig for worms, collect leaves, or look at tiny bugs, the supplies will be ready.

■ **Take a wonder walk.** Preschoolers are filled with wonder. Be sure to stop frequently and to avoid rushing on your walk. Your child might enjoy some binoculars to enhance her sightings. My grandmother used to keep bird and flower guides in her pocket to help us identify wildlife. Look high to observe a bird's nest or look down on the ground to spot an anthill. Bring a bag with handles for carrying ease to collect curiosities (such as colored leaves or dandelion fluff) to reexamine and share later at home. Follow a sound to see where it is coming from; you might find a squeaky swing on the playground or a duck honking on a pond in the park.

■ **Take a neighborhood tour.** Your child will find lots of places of interest. If you drive, you can go through the car wash with scrubbing brushes on the windows or the post office to buy stamps and mail letters. You might walk around the farmers' market, where your child can use all of his senses. Stop by the bakery to take in the inviting smells, eat samples, and watch the strange machinery. Take advantage of an exciting holiday parade with various sounds and fascinating costumes. Encourage questions and colorful responses.

RELATED BOOKS TO READ WITH CHILDREN

Brown, Peter. 2009. *The Curious Garden*. New York: Little, Brown Books for Young Readers.

Hopgood, Tim. 2009. *Wow! Said the Owl*. New York: Farrar, Straus, and Giroux.

Keats, Ezra Jack. 1961. *The Snowy Day*. New York: Viking.

Knowles, Sheena. 1998. *Edward the Emu*. New York: HarperCollins.

Wiesner, David. 2006. *Flotsam*. New York: Clarion Books.

Wood, Audrey, and Don Wood. 1984. *The Little Mouse, the Red Ripe Strawberry, and the Big Hungry Bear*. Auburn, ME: Child's Play.

3

UNDERSTANDING
TIME CONCEPTS

Time—measurable periods when activities or events occur, including past, present, and future occurrences

Three- and four-year-olds care most about what is happening in their world right now, but they also enjoy looking forward to events in the future and hearing stories about the past. Still, they may get a bit confused about different time periods and upset about changes in routines. Although preschoolers develop at different rates, here are some characteristics you might see as they gain an understanding of time concepts:

- Three-year-olds are egocentric; the time they are in at the moment is rather significant for them.
- Three-year-olds' vocabularies contain most of the basic words for time.
- Three-and-a-half-year-olds are using more-complex phrases, such as "just a little while longer."
- Four-year-olds may be able to observe the symbols of the passage of time (four birthday candles), although the time itself is actually invisible.

- Four-year-olds notice if you change the sequence of their routines but may not be aware if you vary the length of time for events.
- Four-year-olds use seasonal words in an appropriate context and are aware of major holidays.

Now let's look a bit closer to see how preschoolers tend to develop their concepts of time and how they might express their understandings in your classroom.

When Ella walks in her classroom, she flashes a huge smile. She tells her friends, "Today, I am four years old! Happy birthday to me! Yesterday my mamma made me a kitty cake." Jordan asks, "When is your party?" Ella happily explains, "At snack. Right after story time." Jordan questions Ella, "Why do you have a kitty cake?" Ella says, "I am getting a kitty for my present. In one week we go to the farm. Mamma says a kitty has to be six weeks old. She cannot leave her mamma before then."

In order for preschoolers to gain a good sense of temporal concepts, it is important for them to have a great deal of experience with time in personal ways. An idea of time comes from their involvement with events such as snack, story time, and Ella's birthday. For Ella and most other preschoolers, who are apt to be quite egocentric, the time they are in right then, the present, is significant to them. Notice how excited Ella is today—her birthday.

When Ella lets her friends know she is going to the farm next week to pick up her kitty, she suggests that she is anticipating a future event and is planning for it. She is also able to recall past events, such as her comment that her mamma made her cake yesterday. Even though three- and four-year-olds have this ability and are quite aware of words telling about past occurrences, such as *last week* or *a while ago*, they sometimes do not get the timing quite right. For instance, Ella's *yesterday* could have been several days ago. Three-year-

Cognitive Development of Three- and Four-Year-Olds

olds sometimes confuse future and past times. For example, Eugene relates, "I'm not going to eat pizza with Tyrone last night."

For preschoolers, time is an abstract concept. It is also intangible. However, Ella may be able to actually see the symbols of the passage of time as she observes the four candles on her birthday cake. The number of candles represents the idea that a year has gone by since her last birthday and she is a whole year older. Of course, the time itself is actually invisible to Ella.

At the end of the day, Mrs. Flipse reviews the events with her preschoolers. They tell her about the highlights of the day while she writes their thoughts next to the daily schedule on an experience chart. Martin tells about making popcorn for snack. Myounna mentions collecting colored leaves during outdoor play time to use later for beautiful collages. Abby explains how they bounced teddy bears on a parachute during music.

Developing a concept of time helps organize young children's experiences and is a basic part of their cognitive development. This skill depends on their capability to understand what comes before and what comes next. For example, Ella knows that story time comes before snack. She also tells Jordan that she can pick up her kitty a week after her birthday. If a child has the ability to order events sequentially, this normally leads to the child's understanding of time intervals. Then preschoolers discover that the day has a predictable sequence.

Preschoolers learn about time concepts naturally as they relate to their daily schedules. For example, Mrs. Flipse's class enjoys sharing meaningful things that happen during specific scheduled times, such as snack, outdoor play, art, and music. When three- and four-year-olds consistently follow a schedule daily, they will feel comfortable about things that occur and learn to mentally represent sequential events. This is important as they learn to develop an awareness of time. When preschoolers are directly involved in routine events at school and home and interact with their personal environments, they learn best.

Earlier in the day, Mr. Sosa promised the four-year-olds that they could get all of the tricycles and scooters out of the shed during outside play time so that they could play car wash with the hose and buckets of water. Imagine their disappointment when he announces that it is raining, so they will not be able to go out at this time. Upset, Bryce says, "That is not fair. You promised!" Trying to placate the preschoolers, Mr. Sosa tells them, "Maybe we can go out later in the afternoon. Right now, let's make some new playdough."

Because many four-year-olds are still egocentric, like Bryce, they see an activity from their point of view. Young children will certainly notice, and sometimes not too kindly, if you change the sequence of their routines. This becomes confusing for preschoolers.

However, you can vary the length of time for events without them usually noticing. An egocentric child feels that time occurs because he is there. In other words, outdoor play time does not really happen unless he is part of the interaction.

Each day, young children are bombarded with constant references to time, hearing "soon," "in a few minutes," "it's nap time," "at two o'clock," "next week," "last month," and "during the summer." As they develop their own sense of time, they become quite secure and show their knowledge about words referring to time. By three years old, the majority of preschoolers have most of the basic words for time in their vocabularies. Ella relates various words to her birthday—*today*, *yesterday*, and *in one week*. Four-year-olds understand past, present, and future words with ease. Silly Sam says, "When I was a baby, I pooped in my pants. But when I grown up, I'll be a cowboy." Birthday girl Ella knows she is four years old right now and is happy to hold up four fingers to represent her age. By three and a half, many children are able to use phrases that are more complex, such as "Shelly has held the doll for a long time now." Myounna, a four-year-old, easily uses *time* in compound words and phrases, such as *outdoor play time*. Four-year-olds are also quite proficient using words such as *minute*, *week*, and *month*.

With a keen grasp of temporal terms, four-year-olds are able to use seasonal words in an appropriate context. Anderson tells his teacher, "I wear a bathing suit to swim in the summer. In the winter, I wear mittens to play in the snow." He is also aware of major holidays, such as Fourth of July and Thanksgiving, and activities associated with them. Four-year-old Anderson shares, "At Thanksgiving, we eat turkey and pumpkin pie."

Three-year-olds enjoy using vocabulary relating to clocks. Fiona looks at the alarm clock in the home area. "Everybody up," she says. "It's twenty o'clock." She scans her play wrist watch and announces, "Ten minutes until breakfast. Don't be late." Preschoolers are not really able to read abstract time-telling devices, such as analog clocks and calendars, until they are older. However, like Fiona, they know these aids help them measure how time passes.

Cognitive Development of Three- and Four-Year-Olds

What You Can Do

- **Facilitate timely transitions.** Develop special signals so that preschoolers will know it is time to end one activity before transitioning to the next one. Not all children may respond the same to transition cues, so tap into their learning styles. For example, five minutes before cleanup time, blink the lights for visual learners, ring a chime for auditory learners, and pat kinesthetic learners on their shoulders.

- **Play beat the clock.** Help children develop a sense of the passage of time. Together decide on a certain number of minutes to work cooperatively to pick up a designated area. Then set a kitchen timer. See if the preschoolers can clean up before the timer dings. Did they beat the clock?

- **Create a simple strip calendar.** Personalize a weekly strip with your class. On large paper blocks, place photos or drawings of interesting things that happen each day: On Monday, Issi's puppy will visit. On Tuesday, we will make applesauce. You can talk about what happened today, yesterday, or three days ago. Make it a meaningful timeline. Don't expect young children to tell the correct day of the week.

- **Record your garden's growth.** Plant seeds indoors or outside. Keep a record of how many days or weeks it takes for the seeds to sprout. Use tally marks and count them. Keep a photographic record of the plants' growth over time.

- **Designate a tree for all seasons.** To help children experience the passage of time and observe how things change, select a particular tree to visit each season. Give the preschoolers sketch pads and crayons to draw how the tree looks to them each season. For example, the tree has bare branches in winter, and it's covered with colorful leaves in the fall. Display the illustrations in a yearlong, seasonal visual timeline. Ask the children to document the seasonal changes over time in a dictated class story.

Other Aspects to Consider—Alerts

- **Preschoolers are not ready to understand abstract time-telling devices.** Until they are nearly six or more years old, when they approach Piaget's stage of concrete operational thinking, it is difficult for young children to read or understand time aids, such as clocks and calendars. Digital clocks have made it a bit easier for some preschoolers to name the time, however, as it appears on the clock face. Although most preschoolers are not really good at telling time, it is important to introduce them to time concepts.

- **The time concept needs to be concrete.** Time words—such as *today*, *tomorrow*, *yesterday*, and *next week*—must be connected to particular activities or events for them to be understandable to preschoolers. At this stage of development, children identify time through meaningful symbols, such as four birthday candles, or identifiable events, such as trick-or-treating at Halloween. Three- and four-year-olds need a recognizable sequence to their daily routines or a defining activity to make time concepts less abstract and more concrete for them.

- **A change in routine confuses a child's sense of timing.** Big events—such as attending preschool for the first time, returning after a vacation, or moving—can make a child's inner time clock go crazy. Changing schedules and the order of events can mess up the comfortable, predictable routine that she expects. If her home routine is upside down, it is helpful to have the school schedule be as normal as possible for consistency. Discuss the new schedule with her so that she will know what to anticipate.

ACTIVITIES FOR PARENTS TO TRY AT HOME

- **Use household activities to explain time concepts.** Explore various time gauges. When you bake brownies together, invite your child to help set the timer. Ask him to tell you when it rings so that you'll know the brownies are cooked. Explain that Daddy will finish mowing the lawn in ten minutes, when the long hand on the kitchen clock reaches straight up at the twelve. For fun, turn an hourglass egg timer over and watch the sand run through while a three-minute egg boils. Ask your child to help move the clothes dryer timer dial all the way to sixty minutes. Check the laundry when it buzzes.

Cognitive Development of Three- and Four-Year-Olds

- **Review with questions.** During a family get-together, enjoy reviewing and anticipating the timing of personal events by asking questions. Your preschooler may not yet be ready to understand all of the units of time, but hearing them can be meaningful. Here are a few suggestions: "When did we go to the beach?" (Answer: Yesterday.) "When do you go to school?" (Answer: Tomorrow.) "When do you put on pajamas?" (Nighttime.) "When will we go to Nana's house?" (On the Fourth of July.)
- **Make clock collages.** Together, search through magazines and newspaper advertising inserts to find various images of timepieces. Cut or tear them out, and glue them on paper to create a collage or booklet. Discuss the characteristics of various watches and clocks—digital with changing numbers or analog with stationary numbers and moving hands. Explore alarm clocks, kitchen clocks, wristwatches, phone clocks, and city building clocks. How are they used?
- **Share family artifacts.** Build on your child's past experiences. So she can have a sense of the passage of time, display special items from her early childhood, such as baby shoes, baby cups, or a favorite cloth book. Share pictures from her baby book. Discuss keepsakes from other family members, such as Mom's baby brush, an older sister's fuzzy teddy bear, or Grandma's baby locket.

RELATED BOOKS TO READ WITH CHILDREN

Carle, Eric. 1999. *The Grouchy Ladybug.* New York: HarperFestival.

Fox, Mem. 1993. *Time for Bed.* Boston: Houghton Mifflin Harcourt.

Harper, Dan. 1998. *Telling Time with Big Mama Cat.* San Diego: Harcourt Brace.

Hutchins, Hazel. 2007. *A Second Is a Hiccup.* New York: Arthur A. Levine Books.

Sierra, Judy. 2004. *What Time Is It, Mr. Crocodile?* Orlando, FL: Harcourt.

Zolotow, Charlotte. 1992. *This Quiet Lady.* New York: HarperTrophy.

DEVELOPING SPATIAL
AWARENESS

Spatial awareness—children's knowledge of their own bodies in space as well as their relationship to objects in space

Three- and four-year-olds can learn about spatial concepts through experience and practice, games, play, and other everyday interactions. Although they do not all develop at the same rate or achieve milestones at the same time, you can observe many of the following characteristics among preschoolers developing their spatial awareness:

- Three-year-olds begin to understand about their orientation within the special boundaries of their environment, such as when they separate from their parents at school.
- Three-year-olds understand the locational prepositions *in, on, under,* and *next to.*
- Three-year-olds love giving directions, but they may be very basic, incomplete, or not exactly accurate.
- Four-year-olds gain an understanding of the special concepts of proximity and distance when they are physically involved.

- Four-year-olds understand the locational prepositions *in front of*, *behind*, *in back of*, *up*, *down*, and *off*. The concepts *above*, *below*, and *at the bottom of* may be more difficult.
- Four-year-olds who are more experienced will build enclosures with blocks and then name the structures.

Now let's look at some scenarios that depict the types of behaviors you might see in your classroom as preschoolers explore spatial concepts.

As the four-year-olds in Mrs. Keyes's class get ready to dance to music, the teacher wants to help them avoid bumping into each other. She hopes to develop their sense of personal space. Mrs. Keyes says, "Please hold your arms out from your sides and move so that you aren't touching anyone. Now slowly turn around. This is your very own bubble space. If you bump your bubble space into someone else's bubble space, you will both pop!" Fascinated, George reaches out with his arm to see how far he can stretch his fingers before they touch Tommy's fingers. "Cool!" he says. "That's pretty far." Thrilled with his awesome experiment, he explains to Mrs. Keyes, "Look, I can see and feel how far my bubble space goes."

A preschooler's knowledge of spatial awareness, lodged in his right brain hemisphere, is related to his own body experiences. Over time, a young child's spatial concepts are developed through his involvement with various concrete situations and experiences with objects and people. For instance, like George's interaction with Tommy, the idea of space for a preschooler is quite egocentric. He needs to be physically involved so he can gain an understanding of the special concepts of proximity and distance. By stretching out the length of his arm and reaching for Tommy's fingers, George feels a sense of self in both tactile and visual ways. As George moves his fingers closer to his friend's while using his body as a reference point, this indicates a four-year-old's ability to think about spatial awareness. When George exclaims that his reach is far, he is demonstrating that four-year-olds realize their sense of distance and space through a relationship between the environment and themselves.

During the first few weeks of child care, it was difficult for three-year-old Lucy to separate from her mom. She cried as her mother left her behind. Now, a month later, Lucy kisses her mom goodbye after they hang up Lucy's jacket in her cubby. She goes to the window, blows her mom another kiss and says, "Later." As Lucy and her mother separate from each other, the three-year-old begins to understand her orientation within the special boundaries of the child care center. She also becomes aware of her mother's movements as she separates from Lucy inside and then outside the environmental space.

In the block center, three-year-old Samuel enjoys building with wooden blocks. He places one long block on top of two others to create a bridge for his crocodile to swim under. Xavier and Joel, four-and-a-half-year-olds, start out by placing one block in front of the other to design a train track. Next they construct a train station by engineering a rectangular enclosure with long and short blocks.

Constructing with blocks provides amazing experiences for preschoolers to explore the concept of spatial awareness as they arrange and rearrange items and observe their positions relative to one another. Block building helps preschoolers understand locational prepositions as they manipulate the materials. Three-year-olds like Samuel can often understand *on*, *in*, and *under*. Three-and-a-half-year-olds tend to be comfortable using *next to*. Four-year-olds, like Xavier and Joel, are often able to use *in front of* as they create structures; however, they can just as easily use the prepositions *behind* and *in back of*. After children have reached four years old, they tend to use *up*, *down*, and *off*.

Spatial visualization occurs when children develop the ability to produce and manipulate images in their minds. Xavier and Joel experience spatial visualization when they create the enclosure for the train station. As three- and four-year-olds first begin to construct, they tend to build incomplete enclosures with their blocks. When they have more experience, they will close up spaces. Next, they give their enclosures names, such as when the four-

year-olds call their structure a train station. Although they may accomplish the engineering feat of designing an enclosure, it may still be confusing for preschoolers to visualize spatially if their toy truck can fit in the block garage they've just built.

Cognitive Development of Three- and Four-Year-Olds

Mrs. Fisher knows that position words with movement prompts are important for her three- and four-year-olds to understand so they will gain a better sense of themselves and objects in space. She shares a beautifully illustrated book, *Elephants Aloft* by Kathi Appelt, in which two young Asian elephants climb into a hot-air balloon's basket. With only one word of text per page, the book shows the little elephants traveling *through* the clouds, *above* the minarets, and *under* rain clouds before jumping *into* the arms of their African elephant auntie. To encourage her preschoolers to actually move their bodies through space and feel it around them by interpreting positional prompts, Mrs. Fisher designates a natural woven laundry basket as the hot-air balloon's basket. The youngsters take turns dramatizing the various prompts on the pages. This also helps them with spatial orientation, which allows them to know where they are and how to get around.

In another classroom, a new student teacher, Ms. Christy, asks three-year-old Ellie, "Do you know where I can find the puzzles?" Happy that she knows where they are, Ellie responds, "Oh, yes. In the little room." Outside, Arati, a four-year-old, asks her buddy Karen, "Where are the balls?" Karen points, "Under the steps by the tiny tree."

Three-year-olds, like Ellie, really love giving directions and are developing quite an interest in spatial details. However, their directions might be basic, incomplete, or not exactly accurate. Four-year-olds, like Karen, use landmarks, such as "the tiny tree" and "under the steps," which note physical locations. Phrases like these help them encode particular locations in the surrounding area. As preschoolers' memory skills develop, they are better able to process, retain, and integrate more physical cues.

By age three and a half, many young children delight in expressing a personal knowledge of location and spatial awareness, such as naming their street. When my grandson Owen was four, he would love to explain, "I live on Sandy Point Lane at Lake Dunmore in Vermont!"

In a preschool's outside play area, Glenn keeps trying to kick a ball into a large open cardboard box. When he finally kicks the ball into the target, his loud four-year-old voice is heard all the way across the playground as he shouts, "Score!" However, Naomi, a three-year-old, uses a much softer voice, meant to be

heard only by Amy, the child standing right next to her, as Naomi tells Amy about the unique, shiny pebble in her hand.

Preschoolers use their bodies (and voices) in different ways in relationship to space and distance. Glenn is kicking the ball *far*, and he wants his exciting message to reach a distance far across the playground. On the other hand, Naomi is *near* her friend and doesn't want her special secret to be heard very far away. Three- and four-year-olds, like Glenn observing the path of his ball, are able to show that they can focus on actions or objects a distance away and then shift their gaze back again without confusion. Also curious about how far he kicked the ball, Glenn asks his teacher to help him figure out the distance. She counts his steps out loud while he paces the distance with his feet.

In Mrs. Gehringer's classroom, the teacher is introducing her preschoolers to some simple mapping skills. She takes them to the playground, not to play but to be "mappers" and look carefully to observe where things are located. A few four-year-olds make sketches using paper on clipboards. Mrs. Gehringer takes some digital pictures while they talk about what they see. Back inside, they discuss how to create a playground map. Several children decide to go to the block area and design a simple map on the floor using different wooden blocks as symbols to depict various pieces of equipment (swings, a climbing frame, and a slide). Some four-year-olds ask the teacher to cut a big piece of green mural paper for the grassy playground. They cut out construction paper shapes to represent the playground equipment, then tape them in their locations. Several four-year-olds use crayons to draw themselves and their friends on the map playing on the equipment. Two boys replicate the tricycle path with a black crayon. Then they all add little toy tricycles and wagons. At group time, the mappers look at Mrs. Gehringer's photos, then take them to their map sites to see if their representations are in the right spaces. The boys decide to move the sandbox and retape this symbol in a slightly different spot.

It is important for preschoolers to have extensive concrete experiences, such as playing on the playground every day, so they can interact with and relate to their surroundings in significant ways. This type of knowledge helps them understand abstract concepts from their environment, such as where to put the playground equipment on a floor or paper map. For example, these real experiences assist the four-year-olds in creating mental pictures so they can refer to them as they draw the pictures of the children to add to their paper playground map. Viewing the photos helps the children create visual maps as they explain how the sandbox is *in front of* the climbing frame. Making the maps expands the young children's experiences as they explore abstract spatial representations.

WHAT YOU CAN DO

- **Play games.** Have fun developing spatial awareness skills through games. Begin playing Near or Far by hiding an item. Then you can say "far" and clap softly if the child is a distance away from the item, or say "near" and clap loudly if she is close to the item. In Red Light, Green Light, children start a distance away from the person designated as the traffic light. The players walk when you say "green light" and then stop for "red light." Who reaches the light first? Giant Steps or Mother, May I? or Doggy, Doggy, Who Has My Bone? are great group games for checking out positions and locations.

- **Manipulate manipulatives.** Encourage preschoolers to use construction materials such as Lincoln Logs, Tinkertoys, and wooden table blocks to design shapes and enclosures. Explore space by building high with Geo D-Stix and Crystal Climbers. Build long or wide with Lego bricks. Twist and turn pipe cleaners and clay to engineer three-dimensional sculptures. Discuss positioning as the children manipulate the various materials.

- **Create an obstacle course.** Preschoolers love to be a part of this spatial challenge! Invite your children to help set up a course using a variety of landmarks (such as a tree, cloth tunnel, construction cone, and pot of geraniums). Encourage them to run around, through, and between the different items. Talk about where they are going. When they've passed the finish line, review where they've been. Running the obstacle course builds their awareness of spatial directions.

- **Use dramatic prompts.** Dramatizing their favorite fairy tales and stories is a wonderful way for young children to explore locational prepositions and the concept of proximity. The goats in "The Three Billy Goats Gruff" story go *across* the bridge and *over* the troll *in* the water and then *down* into the meadow. In the book *Caps for Sale* by Esphyr Slobodkina, the peddler puts one colored cap *on top of* another colored cap. Then the monkeys throw the caps *down* on the ground after the peddler throws his *down*. Children might like to make up and act out their own stories that indicate an awareness of their bodies in space.

- **Encourage movement in space.** A sense of distance is learned through movement. Invite preschoolers to dance around to music. Play Simon Says and Follow the Leader. Freeze Tag allows children to move freely and then stop in space. Parachute play enables preschoolers to run under the chute, puff it up in the air, move around in a circle with it, or put stuffed animals on it and bounce them high up into the air! What a fabulous fun way to gain an understanding of spatial relationships.

OTHER ASPECTS TO CONSIDER—ALERTS

▪ **Monitor poor spatial awareness.** If you notice a child is having this type of difficulty, he may have visual perception problems as well. You might observe him confusing positional language, such as mixing up *on top of* with *on the bottom*. It may be hard for him to follow directions using positional language. He might not distinguish his left from his right. The child might have difficulty judging speed and distance, for example, when a ball is coming in his direction. He may need to work with an occupational therapist, who can provide some remedial exercises and spatially oriented games to play.

▪ **Watch out for signs of physical inactivity.** Physical movement is so important because it affects the cerebellum. This part of the brain plays a role in children's spatial perception. Because movement is a stimulus for cognitive development, you will want to get children moving early instead of sitting. Unfortunately, many young children today are inactive and develop perceptual problems, which can make them appear clumsy. When writing, they have trouble with spacing between the paper and themselves. Letters frequently are different sizes. A child may appear confused between the letters *b* and *d*. The development of body awareness and perception can be a problem for a preschooler with developmental coordination disorder, autism, or cerebral palsy.

▪ **Be tuned into social ineptness.** If a child seems to have a problem with body awareness and spatial perceptions, she may lack knowledge of social boundaries. In her interactions with her peers, she may not be aware of how close or far away to stand from her friends, which may make others uncomfortable. She may even bump into them. You may want to suggest that this child's parents refer her to a physical therapist.

ACTIVITIES FOR PARENTS TO TRY AT HOME

▪ **Do puzzles.** Try working some large-piece jigsaw puzzles together. After looking at the outlines of several pieces, visualize the spaces where they need to go. Let children play around with form boards, which have designated spots for objects of different shapes, and with computer-generated mazes. Help your children develop their ocular-motor task orientation and directional positioning skills with these spatial activities.

▪ **Explore various locations.** Enjoy one-on-one fun by asking your child to find specific things in a particular room at home or at the grocery store. Give clear directions: "Go to your bed, climb up, crawl across your covers, peek under your pillow—surprise, there are your pajamas!" Then switch roles and have your child ask you to find something by giving you directions. This is how preschoolers develop their knowledge of direction, distance, and location.

- **Look at all kinds of maps.** Start simply by introducing your child to something he is familiar with, like a floor plan of his bedroom. Use the computer to find a map of your home in the neighborhood. Look at a computer-generated map of your town or city. Another time, browse through an atlas and find your state. Of course, your child will no doubt really love using a globe to find different locations around the world. With all of the maps, discuss distances by using words such as *way over there*, *below*, and *next to*. These introductions will expose your child to spatial representational systems.

- **Create a scavenger hunt.** Create a little pictorial map of a small area, such as the living room, for your child to follow. Give verbal clues about the items in that space: "Walk ten paces. Where are you?" The child should be at the sofa. "Look under the cushion for the next clue." As the child continues the hunt, encourage her to ask questions too. Make the hidden treasure a treat to enjoy together, such as reading a brand-new book or baking cookies.

- **Have a swinging sing-along.** Singing action songs provides exciting opportunities to explore spatial orientation skills that enable your child to understand and execute requests. Some superb movement songs are "The Hokey Pokey"; the nursery rhymes "London Bridge Is Falling Down," "Jack and Jill," and "The Grand Old Duke of York"; and the perfect song for body awareness, "Head, Shoulders, Knees, and Toes." These are good exercises for Mom and Dad, too!

RELATED BOOKS TO SHARE WITH CHILDREN

Appelt, Kathi. 1997. *Elephants Aloft.* San Diego: Voyager.

Ayers, Katherine. 2007. *Up, Down, and Around.* Cambridge, MA: Candlewick.

Carle, Eric. 1985. *The Secret Birthday Message.* New York: HarperCollins.

Cole, Henry. 2014. *Big Bug.* New York: Little Simon.

Dillemuth, Julie. 2015. *Lucy in the City: A Story about Developing Spatial Thinking Skills.* Washington, DC: Magination Press.

Fleming, Denise. 2012. *Underground.* New York: Beach Lane Books.

Fox, Mem. 2006. *Whoever You Are.* New York: HMH Books for Young Readers.

Hutchins, Pat. 1971. *Rosie's Walk.* New York: Aladdin.

Hutchins, Pat. 1997. *Shrinking Mouse.* New York: Greenwillow Books.

Slobodkina, Esphyr. 2002. *Caps for Sale: A Tale of a Peddler, Some Monkeys, and Their Monkey Business.* New York: HarperCollins.

Sweeney, Joan. 1998. *Me on the Map.* New York: Dragonfly Books.

5

DEVELOPING PROBLEM-SOLVING SKILLS

Problem solving—a way of thinking through the specifics of a problem in order to arrive at a solution

As preschoolers grow and develop, they get better at trying different solutions when the first one doesn't fix their problem. As three- and four-year-olds experiment, you might observe some of the following characteristics in their problem-solving approaches:

- Three-year-olds are apt to see a problem if it occurs in the immediate environment.
- Three-year-olds often base their ideas and workable solutions on past experiences.
- Three-year-olds may leave their problem if it becomes too frustrating for them to solve.
- As their vocabulary increases, four-year-olds are able to explain their experimentations and solutions.
- Because their thinking skills are more complex, four-year-olds are able to contemplate objects or people that are not physically in front of them.

- As four-year-olds become more patient, they are able to explore numerous ideas and solutions until they find one that is workable.

Now let's consider some scenarios that show how preschoolers in your classroom might explore different options for problem solving.

Preschoolers are involved in the problem-solving process all day long every day. For example, when Martin observes that it is raining outside and decides to wear his slicker instead of a jacket to school, he solves a problem based on what he sees. Natalie has a problem too. Her best friend Heather is playing with a puzzle, but Gillian is sprinkling gold glitter all over Cinderella's coach. Who should she play with? How will she decide?

When I was visiting a community preschool in old Beijing, China, I witnessed a delightful problem-solving event outdoors. The teacher had a big basket of nuts that the three-year-olds had gathered the day before. She told the children she was going to play a game and scatter all of the nuts at one time onto the playground. They were to pick up as many as possible quickly and place them in the basket. With a whoosh, the nuts were scattered! Laughing and chasing after the nuts, some three-year-olds picked them up in one hand, while others held them in two hands. A few cradled nuts in their arms. One child captured many nuts in a depression that occurred when she held up the bottom edges of her apron-like smock, which was typical clothing in her Chinese preschool. After the preschoolers returned with their nuts, the teacher asked the children which gathering process they thought worked well. They were intrigued with carrying the nuts in their smocks and wanted to try that idea. The little girl told the class she had seen her mom gather fruit just like that in her apron.

Often, solving a problem is necessary so that the children can get on with their day. Frequently, it is exciting and a great way to sharpen their thinking skills. Three-year-olds, like Martin and the preschoolers on the playground, are more likely to recognize problems if they occur in their immediate environment. Three-year-olds frequently rely on their senses for things they can see (such as the rain) or

touch (such as the nuts) to help them with the problem-solving process. Their problem-solving and thinking skills are often based on actions and the children's perceptions. For example, all of the preschoolers were actively involved by running after the scattered nuts and physically scooping them up. The one girl perceived that her mother's method—placing objects in her apron—seemed quite workable, so she adapted it. Then, after trying several ways to solve the problem, the children could see that the turned-up smock seemed to be the most efficient solution. It really works best for three-year-olds to solve problems when they are related to situations and things that they can actually see and feel. And, of course, they need to be interested in solving the problem as well.

In another classroom, Déjà and Antonia are carrying open plastic jars of tempera paint to the art table when Déjà drops hers. The thick paint rapidly spreads on the tile floor. Worried, Antonia says, "How do we clean this up?" Déjà suggests, "Paper towels." The three-year-olds find that this just smears the paint around. Antonia grabs a wet sponge, but then the paint mixes with the water and makes a sloppy mess. Déjà frowns and says, "Gushy!" Their teacher, Ms. Gupta, observes the girls' frustration. She asks, "What do you suppose might happen if you put some sand on top?" The girls scoop up some sand and then mix it with the liquid paint. When dry sandy paint crumbs appear, both girls smile. Déjà exclaims, "Now we sweep it up. Like the sand that spills out of the sandbox!"

Using a variety of materials, three-year-olds frequently use a trial-and-error process as they develop their problem-solving skills. Although wiping with paper towels and using a wet sponge seemed like good ideas to clean up the thick paint, unfortunately they did not work too well. At times, three-year-olds become rather frustrated when their attempts are unsuccessful, as noted by Déjà's frown and "gushy" exclamation. If they become too baffled, some three-year-olds may simply walk away from the problem. On a positive note, three-year-olds often can reach a much higher problem-solving level if an adult, like Ms. Gupta, or a friend can give them clues or ask a type of question that allows the preschoolers to figure out the actual solution themselves. Three-year-olds often build their ideas and workable solutions on past experiences they've had, as when the girls remembered that they had swept up the sand with a brush and dust pan.

Mrs. Corsillia's room has a giant playhouse, which consists of a wooden structure with tunnels underneath, steps on one side, a slide on another side, and four walls high enough to enclose the large carpeted platform over the tunnels. Several four-year-old boys decide they want to build rooms in the playhouse. They have carried wooden blocks from the construction center in a plastic pail and a laundry basket. As they take blocks out of the basket and begin to carry them up the steps, Mrs. Corsillia stops them. She explains, "I'm afraid you might fall with your hands full. Let's see if you can find a safer way to move the blocks up easily into the giant playhouse."

Mrs. Corsillia thinks this is an excellent time to introduce the four-year-olds to the steps in a problem-solving process. Their problem is already identified. She suggests the boys brainstorm some safe ways to easily move the blocks. Bruce says, "Hey, we could push them up the slide." He demonstrates this. They decide this is not very safe. Dewan offers an idea. "How about a guy on the floor hands blocks up to a guy in the playhouse?" Two boys try this out. They agree that it is too slow. After thinking a while, Paul suggests, "We could tie a rope to the bucket's handle and then pull it up with the rope. My grandpa does that at his barn." Mrs. Corsillia adds, "He probably uses a pulley with his rope." After getting a jump rope, the boys try this idea. While exploring the three solutions and examining them, the boys select the bucket idea. "It's cool. The bucket gets a lot of blocks up at a time." The four-year-olds have lots of fun implementing their chosen solution and building rooms with the blocks in the giant playhouse. When Mrs. Corsillia evaluates their solution with them, they all smile and give a thumbs-up sign! Paul boasts, "We are great problem solvers."

Four-year-olds really enjoy listening to their peers' ideas. Because they are now more able to look at ideas from the viewpoint of others, they like solving problems and working cooperatively. Interacting together to find solutions that appear to be workable, four-year-olds are willing to patiently discuss and try out various suggestions. With an increased vocabulary, four-year-olds are able to explain their problem-solving experimentations and solutions. Because their thinking skills are more complex, four-year-olds are able to contemplate objects or people that are not physically in front of them, as when Paul explained about his grandfather using the pail and the rope. With lots of practice, four-year-olds learn to select from a variety of solutions.

When Christian was at the beach, he watched some scuba divers. Back at preschool, he is now trying to locate some water equipment in the dramatic play center. He finds big sunglasses to use for goggles. Three-year-old Christian spies a milk carton in the kitchen area. With a huge smile, he sticks it partially under his elastic waistband in the back of his shorts. He announces, "My air tank!" Then he pretends to swim off to show his scuba outfit to his friends and his teacher.

Sometimes a problem will arise because an item is not available. Preschoolers might need to find a substitute. As they attempt to solve a problem like this, three-year-olds frequently use their imaginations and thinking skills in clever ways, as when Christian uses a milk carton for an air tank. Full of excitement, they enjoy showing everyone how their make-believe creations operate.

Sometimes, three-year-olds simply get handed a problem. Because Aaliyah easily pulls her foot out of her boot, it seems logical to her that she should be able to push her foot back into the boot. But that doesn't seem to work. She tries and tries again, becoming more and more upset. At times, three-year-olds, like Aaliyah, seem able to focus on just one solution, sure that it is the only answer, even when it is illogical and doesn't work for them. They center on a single phenomenon. For instance, Aaliyah isn't able to perceive a second solution, such as pulling open the Velcro ankle strap to make room and allow her foot to slide right into the boot.

In the clay area, Jack is faced with a different type of problem. Every time he struggles to place the big round head on his clay sculpture, it topples over. Persistent, yet flexible, the four-year-old tries several ideas—pinching the clay head and patting it into a cube. Finally, Jack makes a fist and pounds on top of the round head, saying "Bam, bam, bam! Now you are stuck together."

Using his executive functioning, he is able to regulate his attention and apply his cognitive thinking skills as he solves a problem. More patient than three-year-olds, four-year-olds are willing to explore numerous ideas until they find one that is workable.

The problem-solving process commonly involves critical-thinking and creative-thinking skills. Creative thinking encourages the problem solver to see different ways to do things, brainstorm novel ideas, and use materials in brand-new ways. Along the way, the problem solver might make mistakes as he experiments and takes a few risks. Creative thinking in problem solving occurs when the preschooler is able to be flexible and can look at numerous items or situations in diverse ways, like Christian's scuba-diving equipment.

As a People-to-People delegation leader in Cuba, I toured a preschool center in Havana. I brought boxes of sidewalk chalk for the children. The four-year-olds knew that regular chalk was used to write on the blackboard, but sidewalk chalk was new to them. They took the boxes outdoors, where they brainstormed many creative ways to use the large sticks of chalk. A group of girls, holding dolls, thought it would be fun to draw furniture

Cognitive Development of Three- and Four-Year-Olds

for the dolls because they didn't have any. They really loved that if they didn't like the way a bed looked, they could erase it and make changes or add stripes on top of a solid bedspread. At times, the boys noticed planes flying overhead. After making several sugges-tions, they treated the sidewalk like a long piece of drawing paper. They drew military planes at

the top and made green palm trees below them. Next, a boy decided to use a chalk stub like a bomb and blow up the trees. After it shattered, the others yelled for him to stop because they wouldn't have any chalk left to draw with!

When preschoolers use their critical-thinking skills to help them solve problems, they need to separate ideas into various parts and then analyze them. They may be looking at such things as similarities, differences, categories, and sorting.

After rest time, Mr. Zack's four-year-olds love to play a spontaneous game called Shoes. Each child puts one shoe in the center of the circle. To help the children practice their critical-thinking skills and work on problem solving, Mr. Zack asks lots of questions, such as "How do the shoes look different?" Answers might be laces, buckles, or colors. "Which shoes are big? Can you sort out the sneakers? Which ones are running shoes?" And finally, "How can you get your shoe on?" The best part is that the preschoolers are now all ready to go outdoors after nap time!

What You Can Do

■ **Ask helpful questions.** To encourage children to focus on their problem or finding different solutions if they seem stalled, ask them open-ended questions, such as "What would happen if . . . ?" You can follow up with questions that require them to think creatively or critically, such as "What might happen next if you . . . ?" Questions like these help scaffold the children's problem-solving process to a higher level of thinking.

- **Encourage experimentation.** Provide a place in the classroom where the children can freely experiment with materials for a number of days in an unhurried manner so they can brainstorm. Add all types of odd objects that they can put together in many diverse ways. For example, they might use foil squares, wooden beads, and pipe cleaners to create space aliens, a queen's necklace, or a butterfly in a cocoon. What else?

- **Take advantage of the teachable moment.** Have the children work together to solve daily problems. For instance, coming in from the playground on a sunny day, the preschoolers might complain, "We are too hot! How can we cool down?" Consider all suggested solutions, such as eat Popsicles, drink cold water, make paper fans, sit in the shade, or spray feet with the hose. Vote and select an idea. Try it out. The children feel important when their opinions are considered!

- **Create a class obstacle course.** Springing from the children's interest, this gives them a shared objective for collaborative problem solving. Starting with a blank space (indoors or outside), the preschoolers can brainstorm materials to use, such as boards, a balance beam, cones, and a sign. Then they must determine the types of locomotion they will use, such as walking, crawling, using a tricycle, or a combination. Finally, they have to select rules, which

might be to traverse the course two at a time, go backward at certain spots, or stop at stop signs. And the obstacle course can be easily changed if they need a bigger challenge. This activity is guaranteed to inspire lots of creative fun!

- **Investigate things that roll.** Encourage the preschoolers to use their critical-thinking skills to solve this problem. They can use an indoor or outside slide to test out their suggestions. See how many items they can collect that will roll down a ramp or a slide. They might try items such as a ball, an orange, or a Tinkertoy. Which one will roll fastest, slowest, and silliest? They may wish to draw a chart showing their suggestions and solutions.

Cognitive Development of Three- and Four-Year-Olds

Other Aspects to Consider—Alerts

- **Don't rush to solve a child's problem.** It might seem easier for you to fix things for a child. Instead, step back and evaluate whether the child is able to do it. As long as the problem is appropriate and he is not overly frustrated, allowing the child to continue will help him learn important problem-solving skills and build resiliency. You may wish to guide him and give him support with clues or questions.

- **Explore why a child is avoiding challenges.** "It's too hard!" How often have you heard this cry? When a child constantly approaches an adult with this fixed mind-set, strive to understand why. Is she afraid of failure? Is she afraid of making mistakes? Help the child work on problems as they arise so that she gains confidence and feels empowered as she builds her problem-solving skills. You might consider pairing the hesitant child with a successful problem solver.

- **Turn a mistake into a positive.** When you make a mistake as you try to solve a problem (such as spilling an overflowing box of figurines after you just cleaned them up from the floor), ask the children to help you figure out another way to do it. It is reassuring to them to know adults make mistakes too. Turning your blunder into a learning experience shows them how to persist with problem solving and turn their mistakes around.

Activities for Parents to Try at Home

- **Conduct hands-on explorations.** Offer your child curious items that he can use to practice his problem-solving skills. You might start with magnets and have your child try out various items that would and would not be attracted to the magnet, such as paper clips and plastic buttons. Invite him to find other items in the house, make predictions, and try them out. Label one container *yes* and another container *no*, and ask your child to place each item in the appropriate container after trying it with the magnet. Encourage comparisons, and ask him to explain why he thinks the items are or are not attracted to the magnet. You could also try an experiment with a dishpan of water. Ask the child to make predictions about whether items will sink or float, and then discuss why the items behaved the way they did.

- **Put out a call for superheroes.** Encourage your child to use her creative thinking and fantasy-play activities to aid in solving problems. This can help her feel in control by using her superpowers or magic to gain mastery over a situation. For instance, if your child can't go to sleep because she is afraid of evil monsters with light sabers, put her superpowers to work.

If she is motivated, she might engineer her own protective device by covering a wrapping-paper tube with fabulous light-reflecting aluminum foil, or she might craft a small paper-towel tube into a saber by covering it with superhero stickers.

- **Model problem-solving skills.** Throughout the day, identify problems that occur naturally. Talk aloud about what you are doing to solve them, including what works and what doesn't. Talk about your solutions. Ask your child for suggestions, too. You might say, "Oh, I spilled the milk. I wonder if I should use a sponge or paper towel to clean it up. What do you think?"

- **Build creative items.** Your young child will love to design and build using interesting small-scale supplies, such as empty thread spools, small boxes, scrap wood, buttons, and cotton balls. He could also search through catalogs and magazines to find pictures of toys, furniture, and people. And don't forget glue, markers, and scissors. Using small items, your child can use his creative problem-solving skills and fine motor skills to engineer products such as dollhouse furniture, a space station, or a toy store. This is a great rainy-day project.

- **Think outside the box.** Invite the whole family to play. Take a large cardboard box and brainstorm together. How many ways can you use this box? You might open it up to create a tunnel, pop out of it like a jack-in-the-box, or pull it over your head to make a cave. Next share a medium-size box, such as a cereal box. What could you use this for? You might make a shadow box, a doll's bed, or a mailbox. Then get a small box about the size you use for giving jewelry gifts that is covered with colorful paper. See how good the problem solvers are with this tiny box. It might become a house for lady bugs, a stamp box, or a treasure box. Don't get boxed in with your thinking!

Related Books to Read with Children

Henkes, Kevin. 1993. *Owen.* New York: Greenwillow Books.

Jeffers, Oliver. 2011. *Stuck.* New York: Philomel Books.

Palatini, Margie. 1999. *Moosetache.* New York: Hyperion Paperbacks for Children.

Rohmann, Eric. 2007. *My Friend Rabbit.* New York: Square Fish.

Willems, Mo. 2007. *There Is a Bird on Your Head!* New York: Hyperion Books for Children.

Teacher Resource Book

Miller, Susan, and Barbara Backer. 2000. *Problem-Solving Kids: Creating Self-Directed, Problem-Solving Students.* Torrance, CA: Totline.

6

EXPLORING CREATIVITY
THROUGH ART

Creativity—the ability to form original concepts through the use of imagination, experimentation, and discovery

Preschoolers explore their creativity in many ways throughout the day. This chapter focuses on creating with art, but opportunities arise when young children solve scientific and mathematical problems, engage in dramatic play, sing or play music, write a story, and create an exciting new snack. The following snapshots highlight some of the behaviors that three- and four-year-olds tend to demonstrate as they learn to express themselves creatively.

- As three-year-olds develop improved eye-hand coordination, they can begin drawing recognizable shapes, such as circles, ovals, crosses, triangles, and squares.
- Three-year-olds might like to pull apart a chunk of clay and then create something else, such as rolling a long piece into a snake.

- Three-year-olds can become fascinated by tearing an assortment of paper into pieces, then gluing them down to create a collage.
- Four-year-olds may not include features in their drawings, such as ears or necks. This is not because they don't see these features, but because these features don't currently impress them.
- Four-year-olds tend to be interested in adding things to their clay creations, such as buttons to decorate a clay snowman sculpture.
- Four-year-olds like to show off their mastery of using scissors to cut paper and fabric for collages.

Now let's examine some scenarios that show the kinds of behavior you might observe in your classroom as preschoolers develop their creativity through art.

Ms. Teneshia's preschool classroom environment is conducive to inspiring the children's creativity, particularly in the art center. A double easel for painting is always available. The preschoolers have easy access to a wide variety of art media on low open shelves and in see-through containers. There is an area for clay work and a table for drawing, pasting, and painting. At the children's eye level, there is a huge bulletin board and shelving to display the children's creations.

A young three-year-old, Danny, is painting at the easel today. He is creating a large circle with red paint. He begins experimenting with painting additional red circles. He decides to add more lines that look like crosses. Pretty soon, the large easel paper is saturated with red shapes created in thick, wet, red paint.

On the other side of the easel, Faith is painting a picture of herself talking with her mom. Faith, a four-year-old, creates a large circle for her head and a smaller oval body with lines for her arms and legs. When she adds a cross for her nose and blue circles for her eyes, Faith exclaims, "Oh, I am crying," as the blue paint drips down her face. She adds, "I am sad." When she paints her mother, Faith adds big yellow circles to several fingers on each hand. Faith tells Ms. Teneshia, "These are Mommy's beautiful rings."

At the table, two preschoolers are creating artwork with thick crayons. Three-year-old Aria draws a huge circle representing a head and then adds two lines coming out of the bottom of the head to symbolize legs. After she finishes her drawing, Aria smiles as she tells Ms. Teneshia, "That's you!"

Owen, a four-year-old, uses a green crayon to draw a picture of himself in the middle of the paper, and then at the top right, he draws his dachshund puppy, Bruno, as a brown oval. Owen draws a round purple ball at the bottom of the paper. Earlier, Owen and Ms. Teneshia were talking about their pets, so Owen decided to draw a picture story. He describes it to his teacher. "This is me and my Bruno. We are playing fetch with a ball."

For young children, like these preschoolers in Ms. Teneshia's class, expressing themselves creatively with paint, crayons, and other art media is exciting and fun. These satisfying experiences motivate the children to want to continue exploring and experimenting with color, textures, shapes, and design to find new ways to creatively express their feelings. As young children develop their artistic skills, their creativity evolves. They pass through many fascinating stages, just like the three- and four-year-olds in Ms. Teneshia's class.

As three-year-olds develop improved eye-hand coordination and fine motor skills in the basic forms stage, they will begin drawing recognizable shapes, such as circles, ovals, crosses, triangles, and squares. Like Danny, they enjoy practicing these geometric symbols over and over.

After this stage, three-year-olds tend to draw symbols that are visual representations of something the children consider important. Most often, this representational art is a person, usually with a big circle head and two lines for legs or the body, which sort of looks like a tadpole. As the child is drawing, she may name her artwork, such as when Aria announces, "That's you!" to Ms. Teneshia. Naming her art is exciting because it indicates that the three-year-old is thinking about the mental picture she has created.

In the pictorial stage, four-year-olds tend to start creating art that appears more realistic. A child may add details that she remembers and that seem important to her, such as when Faith paints her mom's gold rings as oversized yellow circles. Still slightly egocentric, four-year-olds represent heads with large circles because heads are used for talking and eating, and these actions are important to the children. If a feature is not included (such as an ear or a neck), that doesn't mean the artist does not see it, but rather that it just isn't quite as impressive right now. The four-year-old uses graphic symbols to represent various objects, as when Faith uses circles for her head and her mom's rings and Owen uses an oval for his dog, Bruno. Four-year-olds are apt to adapt their artwork to incorporate mistakes, such as when Faith turns her dripping blue paint into tears. They also visually represent different thoughts and emotions, as when Faith indicates that her crying figure is sad.

Four-year-olds are eager to talk about and draw or paint experiences that relate to themselves, their family, or their friends. For example, Owen and his teacher shared a conversation about their pets, which motivated Owen to create a crayon drawing about him playing ball with his dog, Bruno. In Owen's drawing, the three representations are randomly placed on the paper in a way that makes them appear spatially to float on the page, which is typical for four-year-olds. At four, children begin to tell more-complex stories about their drawings. They also develop a sense of ownership about their creative artwork, as evidenced by Owen's reference to "me" and "my" Bruno. At this stage, preschoolers love to use colors. However, they are not overly concerned if their color choice is an appropriate representation. For instance, although Owen colored Bruno brown, he created

his own image all in green! I once taught a four-year-old girl who drew and painted everything in purple. Why? It was her favorite color!

However, creativity involving art is more than just experimenting with paint and crayons, as the children in Mrs. Kimbel's class demonstrate. Because it is such a beautiful day, Mrs. Kimbel, the children, and the VIPs (very important parent volunteers) move several activities outdoors. At the clay table, three-year-old Stephanie enjoys pulling little pieces off a big ball she has made. Then she rolls lots of tiny balls. Next, Stephanie rolls the little balls into a long snake. Whereas three-year-olds like to pull clay apart and then create something else, four-year-olds are far more interested in adding to their creations. Lemar makes a clay ball and walks around the playground. He grabs some grass and sticks it on the top for hair. Then he pushes in two pebbles for eyes. Lemar explains to Mrs. Kimbel, "I made a puppet." Extending his experience, she asks, "Can it talk?" Searching the ground, Lemar smiles and adds an acorn for a mouth. The puppet says "Hello!" to the teacher. Using their imaginations, preschoolers are able to create with intention.

Knowing how curious her preschoolers are, Mrs. Kimbel sets up a wooden frame with Plexiglas inside. After two children put on smocks, Mrs. Kimbel offers primary color finger-paints to them so that one child can work on each side. Very excited about using these

Cognitive Development of Three- and Four-Year-Olds

tactile materials in a novel way, three-year-old Penelope is thrilled to slide her right-hand fingers up and down with the yellow fingerpaint. She then adds blue with her left-hand fingers and squeals with delight as the layers of colors mix and change to green. To Penelope's surprise, she can see her friend's fingerpainting through the acrylic plastic. Laughing, they both make slippery, colorful, see-through lines and circles that keep changing each other's artwork. It is obvious that as preschoolers experiment with a variety of media and tools, they truly enjoy the creative process more than the final product.

The day before, several four-year-olds had begun to weave sticks and long dried grasses in the chain-link fence. At the time, they told Mrs. Kimbel they wished that their weaving could have colors. Today, after searching through the art bins, the children bring ribbons, yarn, braided trim, and crepe-paper streamers outside. The preschoolers work together to push and pull the weaving materials through the holes. As they look at the natural materials and the colorful items all together on the fence, it gives them an opportunity to discover how the parts relate to the whole. An exciting creative activity, such as this fence weaving, encourages the children's divergent thinking as they discuss novel solutions and make interesting connections without the pressure of a right or wrong way to do something.

Preschoolers really love to take things apart and put things together. Creating collages meets this need perfectly. Refining their fine motor skills, three-year-olds are fascinated by tearing an assortment of paper into small or interestingly shaped pieces to glue. Four-year-olds, however, like to show off their mastery of using scissors to cut magazine pictures, beautiful papers, lovely laces, and fabric.

Three-year-old Reiley decides to create his collage on red construction paper. With great joy, he squeezes a massive amount of white glue on the paper, then smooshes on his little torn papers in a random design while totally enjoying the entire creative process. Yin, a four-year-old, does some creative thinking and decides to select a cereal box as the base for her collage. After she has cut her pretty collage materials into pieces with scissors, she now gets to choose from many items—paste, staples, tape, string, and ribbon—to stick things together.

By expressing their understanding of art media, preschoolers can make their creative thinking and ideas come alive and become visible.

What You Can Do

- **Keep the media at the easel fresh and exciting.** After the preschoolers have had enough time to try several colors of paint, you can inspire creativity by rotating in some new colors. White is especially fun. Add various textures to the paint, perhaps using soap powder or coffee grounds. Change the type of surface, experimenting with materials such as construction paper, cardboard, or open paper bags. Supply a variety of items to try as brushes, such as a hair brush or even flowers with stems. Ask the children to contribute some novel items as brushes to try out.

- **Investigate illustrations in children's books.** Read and look carefully at the artwork in books illustrated by such artists as Eric Carle, Denise Fleming, Maurice Sendak, Ashley Wolff, and Leo Leoni. Discuss with your preschoolers what media they think the various illustrators used, such as collage, watercolors, pastels, or pen. Compare the use of colors and shapes. Encourage the three- and four-year-olds to create their own storybook pages using some of these creative artistic techniques.

- **Combine art with music.** While your children are drawing or painting, play various types of music (such as jazz, hip-hop, or waltz). Invite them to respond to what they hear and feel: loud and soft sounds, rhythmic beats, high and low notes, or slow and fast refrains. Encourage them to have fun as they create colorful dots, lines, squiggles, and loops representing the myriad of musical sounds.

- **Use digital technology.** Introduce preschoolers to various types of graphic programming. Help to familiarize them with different computer tools. Young children love drawing with color and manipulating images on the computer screen as they use their imaginations. Using a scanner to reproduce their original artwork is exciting and might even lead to several children working together to create a book!

- **Create impressions with handmade stamps.** Paint is perfect for printing. Make a stamp pad with paint-covered paper towels folded in trays. For interesting surprises, use natural items such as flowers, acorns, small branches with leaves, rocks, shells, or interesting plants as printing tools. Roll out a slab of clay. Search for objects in the classroom (such as textured building blocks, a paper clip, or a doll's foot) or outdoors (such as a leaf, a tricycle tire, or sticks) to press into the clay. When the clay dries, paint the impressions to highlight them. Can the preschoolers guess what tool created the impressions?

OTHER ASPECTS TO CONSIDER—ALERTS

- **Keep craft project instructions to a minimum.** When an adult offers a young child structured materials (such as patterns or representational shapes cut out by adults) and combines them with highly structured instructions (fold the circle in half and cut along the dotted line), the child does not have creative input and loses flexibility. Constantly using craft projects implies to the child that his way of creating something may not be good enough. This may squash his self-esteem. If he wants to make a craft project on his own, encourage him to add embellishments or different colors or textures.

- **Accept mistakes.** Paint can drip, paper can tear, paste can dry up, and playdough can become gushy. Young artists should not feel pressured by adults to make a product. Everyone makes mistakes, but young children should not have to worry about how things look. It is more exciting for preschoolers to think creatively about ways to solve problems or modify them. For example, they could turn a tear in the paper into a whale's mouth.

- **Support independent creativity.** You are likely to hear requests such as "Draw the boat for me!" To relieve a child's stressful feelings, invite her to talk about or show you how she thinks the boat might look. Explain that she can choose how to draw it. If she still insists that you draw a model for her, tell her that you  feel it would not be respectful for you to draw on her paper. You might share some pictures in a book about boats and discuss features she might like to try drawing.

ACTIVITIES FOR PARENTS TO TRY AT HOME

- **Have fun mixing colors.** Young children are absolutely fascinated when one color added to another color turns into yet another color right before their very eyes. Try some of these with your child and enjoy some intriguing and colorful discussions. Mix homemade blue and red playdough together. Design sunglass frames by using cardboard file folders, then cutting out frame shapes. Glue on colored cellophane lenses, so your child can check out the colorful world. Your child can layer the glasses to combine lens colors. Surprise! Add food coloring to clear plastic drinking glasses filled with water. Then your child can use an eyedropper to add one color of water a bit at a time to a glass with another color of water to create "wonder water."

- **Display feature photos.** Use technology to encourage your child to focus on things of special interest or particular beauty. Take pictures with an iPad or your cell phone as you take a walk or you interact together. Use your printer to make copies. Then display your photographic art. Talk about similarities and differences in the photos. Discuss shapes and color. Create an album to share your special photos.

- **Do the twist!** A huge part of creating artwork is manipulating materials and enhancing your child's eye-hand coordination. Bending, twisting, and attaching colored pipe cleaners can be marvelous fun. Making designs to create bendable people and animals can be amazing. Tying thick, colored yarn around cones or drizzling white glue on cardboard and placing the yarn in twisty designs looks playful. Twisting sheets of shiny aluminum foil into fierce dinosaurs or elegant crowns takes your child's creative artistic manipulations to the next level.

- **Use media in novel ways.** Explore what happens when crayons are used on sandpaper or corrugated cardboard. Place a rubber band around two or three crayons. Wow! Double and triple line drawings. Hang long butcher's paper on a fence. Using clean plunger-type spray bottles filled with water and then watery colored paints, encourage your child to have fun spray painting a huge mural outdoors. The runny drips and action of the wind will keep changing the painting!

- **Visit the creative artwork of others.** Take photos, make sketches, and talk about sculptures you see on a walk in the park. Visit a local art museum or gallery to see the works of professional artists. Many have programs for young children. Encourage your child to become inspired by art hanging in the library or bank. Ask art students at a high school show to have a dialogue with your child about the media they use, their motivations, and how they feel about their creations.

RELATED BOOKS TO SHARE WITH CHILDREN

Carle, Eric. 2011. *The Artist Who Painted a Blue Horse.* New York: Philomel Books.

dePaola, Tomie. 1997. *The Art Lesson.* New York: PaperStar.

Frazier, Craig. 2010. *Lots of Dots.* San Francisco: Chronicle Books.

McDonnell, Patrick. 2006. *Art.* New York: Little, Brown Books for Young Readers.

Saltzberg, Barnie. 2010. *Beautiful Oops!* New York: Workman.

Spires, Ashley. 2014. *The Most Magnificent Thing.* Toronto: Kids Can Press.

Winter, Jonah. 2002. *Frida.* New York: Arthur A. Levine Books.

7

DEVELOPING MATHEMATICAL THINKING

Mathematics—a study of numbers, quantities, geometry, and measurement, and their relationships

Although young children reach particular milestones in cognitive development at different times and to varied degrees, you might see some of the following tendencies while observing preschoolers' exploration of mathematics concepts in their world:

- Three-year-olds sort and classify objects by just one characteristic, usually by shape first, then color, and then size.
- Three-year-olds use one-to-one correspondence to match objects from one group with items from another to see if the groups are equal.
- Three-year-olds recognize and can name measurable attributes (such as length and width) of items.
- Four-year-olds are able to classify by more than one attribute at a time.

- Four-year-olds can place a small number of objects in order from biggest to smallest and describe what they are doing.
- Four-year-olds can copy a pattern from memory after looking away.

Now let's look at some examples of how the preschoolers in your classroom might develop and demonstrate their mathematical thinking throughout the day.

Every day, Mrs. Patel's preschoolers are busily involved with a large variety of hands-on math explorations related to numbers, matching, sorting, classifying, ordering, shapes, measurement, one-to-one correspondence, and patterns. Their discoveries and concrete experiences are important in helping three- and four-year-olds build and understand mathematical concepts.

It's cleanup time in Mrs. Patel's room. The manipulatives table is a colorful mess with parquetry blocks, table blocks, and bristle blocks all mixed up together. The teacher asks a small group, "How can we sort the different toys?" Nate suggests, "Get the empty toy bins. Put the different toys in their own bins." The preschoolers think that's a good idea. The children each take a bin and begin sorting through the pile to find the specific type of toy they are putting away.

The next day, three-and-a-half-year-old Lyla experiments with a new classification activity. Mrs. Reinecke, a parent volunteer, brought in a basket filled with a collection of tops she was saving—aerosol caps, toothpaste tops, hand-lotion screw tops, butter-tub tops, and detergent-bottle caps. Mrs. Reinecke asks Lyla, "What would be fun to do with the tops?" Lyla thinks for a minute, then smiles and says, "Find my favorite color—yellow." Next, Lyla sorts out all of the yellow tops and creates a long yellow parade. Several four-year-old boys are intrigued with the new top activity. Colton decides to pull out the large tops and then spreads them on the table. Jorge sorts out all of the little tops. Hunter comes along and announces, "Hey! Look at this. Put some little ones in the big ones. Then you have aliens in UFOs."

When children sort and classify various objects by different characteristics, this allows them to create a set of items that have something in common. Classification opportunities, which require children to recognize likenesses and differences, occur naturally throughout the day. At cleanup time in Mrs. Patel's room, the preschoolers identify a categorical classification, which is based on membership in a specific group. In this case, the group is manipulative toys. On the other hand, the children with the top collection use a descriptive classification based on physical criteria, such as Lyla's choice of color and Colton's and Jorge's selection of size as attributes. At first, three- and four-year-olds attempt to sort and classify objects by just one characteristic. They usually classify by shape first, then by color, and next by size. Eventually, they are able to classify by more than one attribute at a time. Four-year-olds tend to enjoy classifying things their own way and can even become rather creative. For example, Hunter demonstrated this when he called the little tops aliens and the large ones UFOs.

In Ms. Becky's room, two best buddies are teasing each other about who is tallest. Ms. Becky tells them, "Stand back to back." Then she measures with her hand on their heads. She announces, "Chase is the tallest. He is taller than Mateo." Wyatt joins them and boasts, "I think I am tallest." Ms. Becky gets the long mirror from the dramatic play center and turns it sideways. The three boys line up, look at their reflections, and then sort themselves out by height. "Wow!" laughs Wyatt. "I am the shortest." Ms. Becky smiles at the boys and then declares, "Wyatt is tall, Mateo is taller, and Chase is the tallest."

Over in the kitchen area, several girls are playing Goldilocks, so they are searching for certain sizes in a stack of bowls. Three-year-old Saura explains to Ms. Becky that, as in the story "Goldilocks and the Three Bears," they need a little bowl for Baby Bear, a middle-size bowl for Mama Bear, and a big bowl for Papa Bear. It is easy for the girls to find the biggest and littlest bowls, but they struggle to identify the middle-size bowl and place it in the ordered sequence.

Ordering and seriating activities happen spontaneously in the classroom. When the children order things, it helps them make comparisons based on size and develop the concepts of *more* and *less*. For instance, this occurs when Chase and Mateo stand next to each other. As the four-year-old boys talk about and sort themselves out according to their height comparisons in the mirror, they move into a sequence that gradually reflects smallest to largest. This enables the preschoolers to observe ordered size relationships. Four-year-olds use comparative language and concepts—such as height, length, and size—when they look for similarities and differences among objects. Seriation involves noticing differences among objects and then arranging them according to the differences. The girls who are trying to place the three bears' bowls in order are learning that objects in the same group may have different degrees of a characteristic and that arranging them in a series makes the degrees more obvious. Three-year-olds are already aware of and use words that imply size and quantity relationship, as indicated by their search for big and little bowls.

Ms. Anderson, the assistant teacher in another classroom, is setting out four watercolor paint boxes. There are four chairs at the art table, and she asks Asher to place a smock on each chair. Then Ms. Anderson gives him a container of watercolor brushes and requests that he put one brush on every box. Nearby, Elizabeth decides to take the baby dolls outside for a ride in the stroller. She places one hat on each doll's head.

One-to-one correspondence occurs when a child like Elizabeth matches objects from one group with items from another, such as the dolls and the hats, to see if the groups are equal. Ms. Anderson is helping Asher develop his sense of one-to-one correspondence by pairing two groups of items, such as the chairs with the smocks and the paint boxes with the brushes. That way, he can see if they have the same number. Both of these preschoolers are beginning to develop their number skills as they attempt to figure out how many items from each group are needed for a match.

When Ashlyn walks into the classroom, she is so excited. She enthusiastically holds up three fingers and tells everyone she sees, "I'm three years old! Today is my birthday!" During snack she points to her cake. "See. Three candles for me." The concept of three is important to Ashlyn. She knows how to count to three out loud.

In the music center, Edward has five drums spread out on the floor. Like many three-year-olds, he is not yet able to match number words with the items being counted. As a result, Edward counts the drums using skip counting, or missing an object while continuing to count. Edward counts, "One, two, three," then skips the fourth drum, and counts "four" for the fifth one. Naturally, this gives him an incorrect count. On another try counting the drums, Edward double counts by counting the same drum two times. When Edward's counting does not match the correct number names to the drums counted, he

Cognitive Development of Three- and Four-Year-Olds

is simply counting by rote. *Rote counting* means preschoolers can say the numbers in order, but that doesn't mean they really understand numbers or quantities.

In the art center, several boys cover about three dozen stones they have collected with gold glitter glue. After the stones dry, the four-year-olds distribute their make-believe gold in treasure chests (plastic salad boxes). They bury the treasure in the big playground sandbox. When Pirate Blake digs up his loot, he begins to count his pieces of gold. "One, two, three, four, five, six, seven, eight, nine. I'm rich! I have nine gold nuggets," cheers Blake. Dequan puts his gold treasure in two piles. He counts three nuggets and three nuggets. Thrilled, Dequan announces, "I have six chunks of gold!" Blake tells the other pirates, "I have more gold than Dequan."

When a child like Ashlyn holds up three fingers and she understands that this represents the same amount as three candles, she recognizes the concept of number. Counting involves learning the sequence of number names, as Blake has done. Then preschoolers use the numbers to identify quantities of items. Most four-year-olds can count at least up to four. By age four, most young children understand *cardinality*, which is the number of elements in a set of items. Blake demonstrated this when counting his gold nuggets and announcing that he had nine gold pieces; he understood that the last number in the counting sequence indicated the quantity of items in the set. Although adults may be pleased when a preschooler shows he is able to count to twenty by rote, it may not be truly meaningful. The mathematical learning is more developed when children can connect actual objects to the corresponding number. For instance, when Dequan counts the number of gold nuggets in each pile and discovers he has six, he is showing an early understanding of addition.

Another teacher, Mrs. Maloa, is playing a game of patterns with her three-year-olds. She introduces the sequence "clap-clap, clap; clap, clap-clap." She asks, "What did I do?" Martin says, "Clap your hands." The teacher says, "Yes. Can you copy my clapping pattern?" Martin does, and then the preschoolers have fun imitating several more auditory patterns.

At the manipulatives table, a few children notice Mrs. Maloa's big colorful necklace. The beads form a blue-green pattern. She offers them laces and large beads to create their own necklaces, making sure not to supply beads that could be choking hazards. Two girls replicate her pattern, but three-and-a-half-year-old Tina engineers her own design with beads in a pattern of orange-red-yellow, orange-red-yellow.

Mr. D lines up his four-year-olds to take a walk. He arranges them boy-girl, boy-girl. He asks the children about the arrangement. Booth replies, "You made a pattern with us— boy-girl." Mr. D tells them, "Today we're going on a pattern walk. Tell the class when you see a pattern." Right outside the building, Anna exclaims, "Look at the bricks.

Short-long-long-short-long-long." Mr. D invites everyone to use their sketch pads and markers to draw Anna's brick pattern. Many four-year-olds can copy from memory after looking away. Back in the room they discuss the sketches of the patterns they found. Then Mr. D encourages small groups to select various math materials (attribute blocks, parquetry blocks, Cuisenaire rods, and Unifix cubes) to create their own patterns. Booth uses all red attribute blocks and names the shapes in his pattern, "circle-triangle-square-rectangle, circle-triangle-square-rectangle."

Learning about patterns, sequences of colors, shapes, items, movements, or sounds that repeat themselves can help preschoolers see relationships among various elements. An introduction to patterning occurs when children identify a simple existing pattern, as Martin does with the claps and Booth does with the boys and girls in line. At three years old, many children can identify the basic sequence and extract the pattern. Next children learn to copy a pattern, such as the three-year-old girls with the beads and the four-year-olds sketching Anna's brick pattern. Creating their own patterns, such as Tina's colored necklace or Booth's more complex geometric pattern, is more difficult. Many four-year-olds can recognize and name the basic shapes. Preschoolers can observe patterns in nature, dancing, game playing, and stories with delightful repetitive words.

In Ms. Michaels's class, the three-year-olds are excited about using measuring cups, tall pitchers, milk cartons, measuring spoons, and ladles in the sandbox table. As they fill different-size containers, they discover that some hold more sand and others hold less. The next day, Ms. Michaels puts the measuring materials in the water tub. After experimenting for a while, the preschoolers decide to use the tall pitcher to make pretend lemonade with water because it holds more. If they pour the water into the smaller carton, it overflows.

In another area, three-year-old Kiri creates a dinosaur land with the wooden blocks. He wonders which dinosaur is the heaviest, so he puts one on each side of the pan balance scale to see. The Tyrannosaurus rex side tips down. It's the T. rex!

At a nearby table, four-year-old Sophia shares a special doll from home. She shows her friends the Russian nesting doll that her grandmother brought her. They gently pull the top off of each little doll to find a smaller one nesting inside. Then Sophia and her friends order the dolls on the table from smallest to largest.

Cognitive Development of Three- and Four-Year-Olds

Meanwhile, Sean and Brady decide they are going to make a garage out of a cardboard box for their ride-on bus. The four-year-olds opt for measuring the length of the bus by laying down pencils end to end.

Preschoolers learn that measuring involves determining various amounts. Three-year-olds tend to be able to recognize and name measurable attributes (such as length and weight) of items, as the children in Ms. Michaels's class do. Four-year-olds develop their language abilities as they describe measurable properties, such as *big* or *small* for height, area, and volume. Not yet ready to use standard measuring units, resourceful four-year-olds use nonstandard measurement items such as pencils, paper clips, or footsteps to reproduce length or width. Using math in natural ways helps to make sense of things for preschoolers as they begin to understand math concepts.

What You Can Do

- **Infuse music with math.** There are so many great songs and fingerplays that encourage your preschoolers to act out and practice their counting skills. You might try "One Potato, Two Potato," "Johnny Works with One Hammer," "One, Two, Buckle My Shoe," and "Five Little Monkeys Jumping on the Bed." Make up fun patterns for dancing, such as twirl, march, and then clap-clap-clap! Or create cool, intriguing preschool line dances.

- **Do math their way.** Support your preschoolers' spontaneous mathematical discoveries throughout the day. For example, during breakfast at Trinity Head Start when Pablo folds his square napkin he has a wonderful surprise—a triangle! Then Shan shares how to create a folded rectangle. While two girls sit on the floor with their legs spread apart, as they face each other and the soles of their shoes touch, Brianna exclaims, "Look. We made a diamond!" When these amazing discoveries occur during your day, document and discuss them. Take digital photos to share on a poster of math discoveries.

- **Show that math is more than counting.** Although many wonderful counting and number books are available, be on the lookout for math concepts in old favorite stories—such as size in "Jack and the Beanstalk"—and share them with children. In a delightful Caldecott Honor book called *Waiting* by Kevin Henkes, five animal toys wait for marvelous things to happen. But the real surprise is all of the math concepts that are tucked into the cleverly illustrated pages: time, one-to-one correspondence, patterns, subtraction, addition, sequential ordering, problem solving, and of course counting! This book actually makes math fun. See what math concepts you and the children can find in various books.

- **Play some classification games.** At circle time, you might have a conversation about two stuffed animals, such as a bear and a rabbit. What makes them the same? Different? Why?

For another activity, you could share six to eight pictures and invite the preschoolers to classify the items. For example, pictures of a fire and a cup of soup would be hot, and the cold category would include an ice cream cone and a snowman. You might also ask children to find pizza toppings among a variety of cutout magazine pictures or computer clip art. Then they might like to create a big pizza by gluing the toppings onto a round sheet of mural paper. Another option is to ask the children to line up to go home by classifications, such as clothing colors.

■ **Choose computer programs carefully.** Instead of having preschoolers use programs that look like workbooks, try to scout out technology that lets them be in control. For example, foster opportunities for them to control a cursor to draw items on the screen. This encourages them to be active explorers as they engineer what is happening. Computer drawing programs are most appropriate for beginners. These encourage children to create lines, curves, and angles. This enhances their spatial-thinking abilities and gives them instant feedback with a fun medium.

OTHER ASPECTS TO CONSIDER—ALERTS

■ **Don't let your math anxiety show.** Many adults had stressful experiences with math when they were young. They felt pressured to get the right answers. If you had this type of experience, preschoolers may pick up on your apprehension. Now that you are in the role of facilitator, try to emphasize the process rather than the product, especially with young preoperational children. Support their explorations and encourage them to share their ideas. Smile and have fun with them.

■ **Be aware of inappropriate materials.** Children of this age don't gain much from using worksheets that are structured and do not allow them to use hands-on experiences to develop math concepts. Using materials that require drill and rote responses, such as flash cards, calls for little understanding from young children.

■ **Note children's learning styles.** Teach to children's strengths. Preschoolers need lots of practice exploring with math learning materials to develop concepts. For kinesthetic and tactile children, provide a magnetic board with magnetic shapes and numbers. They'll also enjoy using hands-on colored beads for patterning and different sizes of attribute blocks for classification activities. The visual child likes colorful materials, such as Lego bricks, to manipulate. Encourage the children to compare various sizes of containers for holding and pouring water. For the auditory learner, describe what's happening or talk about the shapes in a puzzle. Use tambourines and rhythm sticks to create musical patterns.

Activities for Parents to Try at Home

■ **Encourage creative math cookery.** Young children love cooking experiences, whether they conjure up birthday cakes in the sandbox or decorate a real cake in the kitchen with you! Count out cups of flour to learn about numbers, quantity, and volume. Compare size to see if a tablespoon is bigger than a teaspoon. Hands-on addition occurs as your child pours in two cups of sugar and then adds one more to make three. Create geometric patterns on a sheet cake. You could use round cherries for eyes, a square pineapple chunk for a nose, and a clementine section as the mouth to create a smile; then repeat the pattern all over the cake. And, of course, brush up on one-to-one correspondence as each child gets one plate and one big piece of yummy birthday cake.

■ **Take a shape walk.** As a family project, use colored construction paper to cut out various sizes of geometric shapes. Let each person select a shape. You can walk around the house, neighborhood, or park. Call out your shape when you find a match, for example, "Rectangle— door." Afterward, glue those different shapes on white paper and use crayons to illustrate the items you saw along the way. Later, design imaginative, silly shapes or scary shape pictures to share.

■ **Play a game of twos.** Two—where are you? When you need a quick fun game while waiting at a restaurant or riding in the car, play a game of twos. Search for pairs of something, such as hands, ears, earrings, socks, or seat belts in the front seat. You will be surprised what your child finds. My favorite child-spotted pair was "two nose holes"!

■ **Shuffle and sort for sequential ordering.** When you are doing family activities, going shopping, or going about daily routines, put technology to work and take a series of digital photos. Print these out by classifications. Shuffle each group of photos. Encourage your child to discuss what's happening. See if she can order them in the sequence she remembers. (Set the table, pass the food, and eat; push an empty grocery cart, buy some vegetables, and check out.) Your four-year-old may be able to name what occurred first, second, third, or last.

■ **Fly away.** Preschoolers can't wait to play board games—again and again! Candyland can strengthen counting skills, matching skills, and learning colors. Toward the end of the game, our family loved to estimate how many more squares to go. Spinners enable your child to correspond a written numerical symbol with how many moves to count out. Preschoolers have so much fun shaking the noisy dice and rolling them when it is their turn. With two dice, they count all the dots on the first one and then the second. Although winning may be exciting, your child will really treasure the time spent with you.

Related Books to Share with Children

Dodds, Dayle Ann. 1996. *The Shape of Things*. Cambridge, MA: Candlewick.

Ehlert, Lois. 1997. *Color Zoo*. New York: HarperFestival.

Gág, Wanda. 1928. *Millions of Cats*. New York: Putnam.

Grossman, Virginia. 1995. *Ten Little Rabbits*. San Francisco: Chronicle Books.

Henkes, Kevin. 2015. *Waiting*. New York: Greenwillow Books.

Hoban, Tana. 1997. *Is It Larger? Is It Smaller?* New York: Greenwillow Books.

Hoban, Tana. 1998. *So Many Circles. So Many Squares*. New York: Greenwillow Books.

Katzen, Mollie, and Ann Henderson. 1994. *Pretend Soup and Other Real Recipes: A Cookbook for Preschoolers and Up*. Berkeley, CA: Tricycle Press.

Schlein, Miriam. 1996. *More Than One*. New York: Greenwillow Books.

Wolff, Ashley. 2013. *Baby Bear Counts One*. New York: Beach Lane Books.

8

INVESTIGATING
SCIENCE

Science—a method of observing, testing, and experimenting with things in nature to learn more about the world

f you let young children follow their natural instincts to question and explore, you will see their inner scientists emerge. You might notice some of the following tendencies as preschoolers develop their science investigation skills:

- Three-year-olds are very curious about their bodies and how they function.
- While gardening, three-year-olds will talk about the growth and changes they observe, which helps them understand that plants are living things.
- Three-year-olds begin to realize that light makes shadows.
- Four-year-olds enjoy learning about and visiting real places (the zoo, a greenhouse, an observatory) and pretending to be scientists.
- Four-year-olds become aware that some items sink in water, while others float; however, they believe that heavy items sink and that light ones float.
- Four-year-olds are able to think about how to change the size and shape of their shadows.

Now let's take a peek into some classroom scenarios and see how preschoolers might interact with materials and one another while investigating science inside and outside.

Mrs. Dolgos's preschool classroom is a most welcoming place for young curious scientists. A discovery table is set up with a variety of seeds and nuts. Unbreakable magnifying glasses are available for close observation while children are classifying the items. A pulley system has been set up in the block area for the children to test various physics and engineering experiments. Some baby chicks will be hatching any day in an incubator, so the three- and four-year-olds can observe growth and change firsthand. Charts hanging by the water table share comparisons of sinking and floating items. The library rack is outfitted with research materials—books, magazines, and catalogues all related to seeds, nuts, flowers, vegetables, and fruits. The music center provides an opportunity for the preschoolers to add different seeds and nuts to plastic yogurt containers, so the children can predict which seeds or nuts will make the loudest or softest musical sounds when shaken. The exciting classroom environment invites preschoolers to poke, sniff, listen, taste, and observe as they participate in hands-on explorations and use their critical-thinking and creative-thinking skills while expanding their scientific knowledge.

When I taught preschoolers at the Kutztown University of Pennsylvania Early Learning Center, a four-year-old boy named Dean fell out of his bunk bed at home. He came in one morning with his right arm totally encased in a cast. The children had so many questions for Dean: "What happened?" "Does your arm hurt?" "Was there blood all over?" "Can you take the cast off?" "What are your bones doing now?" We decided to write a list of things Dean and his classmates knew about broken bones. Then they dictated a chart about what they wanted to know about broken bones. Tracy remembered that the class had visited my husband's archaeology lab on campus at Halloween to see the skeleton. The children agreed that Professor Miller would be a good person to ask about bones.

The next morning, we walked over to the anthropology department. Dean's mom brought along his X-rays. Professor Miller encouraged the children to explore their own arms (the flesh was soft) and the skeleton's arms (the bones were hard). They looked at Dean's X-ray pictures to see if they could find the breaks in his bones and where they might be on the skeleton. They tried bending their own arms like a big hinge and then moved the skeleton's elbows; they wanted to see how the bones in the arms moved with the help of muscles. Professor Miller invited the preschoolers to examine their own arms to see what protected their bones. They guessed, "The skin." He asked them also to think about what was under the skin on a chicken leg. They responded, "Meat." He explained that the skin and flesh or meat help to pad and protect the bones from breaking during bumps and falls.

They could see and understand how Dean's cast was now protecting the bones in Dean's arm temporarily until it healed.

Before they left the lab, Professor Miller said he wanted them to be scientists and research a problem. He showed them a skull and had them tap on the top to see how hard and thick it was. He then placed a flashlight inside the skull and showed how they could see the light shining on the side of the skull, but not the top. He helped the children see that the bones on the sides of their heads, just like on the skull they were looking at, were thin and could break more easily. He explained that they should not turn their heads to the side when being thrown a baseball. Four-year-old Gregg volunteered with a big smile, "That's why players wear helmets!" Tracy added, "I wear a bike helmet. If I crash, my skull won't break." Pleased, Professor Miller agreed and asked them to see if they could find other ways to protect their bones.

Dean's broken arm was a matter of interest to all of the children, no doubt because preschoolers, three-year-olds in particular, are very curious about their own bodies and how they function. In using a scientific method to investigate scientific problems or questions, the first step is to gather information, usually by observing and comparing things. Much of this was accomplished when the preschoolers decided to visit Professor Miller's archaeology lab. This was especially exciting for the four-year-olds, who tend to enjoy learning about and visiting real places. Through hands-on explorations of their own arms and the skeleton's bones, the preschoolers were actively involved with gathering information. This helped the three-year-olds think about the internal and external features of their bodies and what they do. They learned that skin and flesh help protect bones. The discussion led them to connect the concepts of *structure* and *function* as they saw how parts of the body help with the body's survival. When the children observed the thin side of the skull and heard about what might happen if it was hit and broken, they were learning about the concept of *cause and effect*. Seeing and feeling the skull's thin and thick characteristics helped the four-year-olds, like Gregg and Tracy, explain these specific properties of an item they had observed as well as how these properties could influence behaviors, such as wearing helmets. With their new information, the preschoolers were thrilled to be asked to pretend to be scientists.

Very excited, the children were anxious to find ways to solve the problem once they were back in the classroom. "What can we use to protect our bones?" they asked. I mentioned that we needed to have a *thinking point*—in other words, something to help us think through the problem. As the teacher, I couldn't allow them to try out solutions on their own bones in case they really broke them. Dean suggested using chicken leg bones as Professor Miller had mentioned. The preschoolers agreed, and several parents boiled lots of chicken leg bones to sterilize them. (I'm sure several families had chicken soup that night!)

The next day at circle time, the children discussed ideas about things to put around the bones. They thought they might want to use things that would be thick or hard. They decided to search in the various centers for things they could use in these categories. I placed labeled charts on two tables for them to record their findings. On one chart, they listed the found items with the characteristic of *thick*: pot holder, paper-towel tube, cotton balls, wool mitten, and Styrofoam meat tray. On the other chart, they listed items that they considered *hard*: aluminum foil, plastic-metal eyeglasses case, tin tea box, wooden ruler, and small section of plastic pipe.

The preschoolers had an opportunity to handle and look over the materials. Then they had questions: "Was the aluminum foil hard enough?" "How would they attach things?" After speculating, they decided to have me write their prediction: "Thick and hard materials can help protect bones from breaking." Continuing with using the scientific method of inquiry, the preschoolers were still gathering information. They began to group the materials by recognizable traits, such as thick and hard.

At three years old, children are usually able to classify things by their function. Four-year-olds in particular tend to find that it is helpful to record information to organize their ideas, and they may contribute to adult-created charts.

After asking lots of questions and making speculations, the next step in the scientific inquiry process is to make a prediction. The children in my class did this and then wanted to test their prediction about the materials. Dean's mom told the young scientists that when he fell off his bunk bed, he hit the floor with great force. From playing with their superheroes, the preschoolers knew that force had to do with speed and power. They talked about what to use that might break a bone with force. After mentioning a baseball and a rock, they decided on a hammer. They tried pounding an unprotected chicken bone, and it broke. That worked!

The children were involved with their experiment over the next few days. They put a bone inside of every designated protective material. At the workbench, different recorders took turns using technology to take photos and sketching drawings of what each bone and the covering looked like after they were hit with the hammer. Their tests were exciting! For example, the aluminum-foil-covered bone broke, but nothing broke in the plastic-metal eyeglasses case. They enjoyed sharing their findings with each other and gluing the pictures of the most successful protections on a poster labeled "Best Ideas." They created a booklet of their drawings to give to Professor Miller so he could see their experiments.

The third step of the scientific inquiry method is testing with an experiment. It is important to give children ample time to explore and check their investigations. Four-year-olds have a real fondness for experimenting with new and different materials. They eagerly engage in cooperatively planned investigations. For three-year-olds, experimentation is a primary method of learning, and they will try various ideas until they find a successful one. The testing step of the scientific inquiry method relates to the evaluation process, which involves gathering documentation, analyzing results, stating conclusions, and reporting results. The preschoolers were enthusiastically involved with evaluating their findings and communicating them with others. The three-year-olds showed they were able to create very simple representational drawings as a form of data, and the four-year-olds were able to record more details on their drawings.

Some scientists like to add an application step to the process, which would broaden the scope of the children's experience. The Early Learning Center preschoolers had an amazing surprise when their student teacher, Mr. Mulderick, invited a number of his athlete friends to visit in their protective gear. The young scientists had a special opportunity to observe, touch, and try on parts of football, field hockey, lacrosse, and baseball catcher's uniforms. They learned the shoulder pads and faceguards were hard. The chest protectors and gloves were thick just like their discoveries! When the players left, the children used crayons, paint, markers, and clay to design their very own protective gear, applying their understanding gained from their experience.

A wonderful spin-off of this scientific project related directly to Dean's broken arm. The preschoolers introduced a No Broken Bones campaign with posters and safety rules, such as "No pushing on the slide" and "No climbing on the jungle gym with flip-flops or cowboy boots." The three- and four-year-olds certainly gained important practical information about their bodies through their scientific experiments in the fields of anatomy and archaeology.

Throughout the year, many scientific experiments occur in Mrs. Hill's program. The preschoolers have fun exploring scientific concepts in physics, botany, geology, and astronomy. One day, four-year-old Sheldon places a number of items he has collected into the water tub. Because all of the red objects go to the bottom, Sheldon centers, or focuses, on this one specific aspect to the exclusion of all other attributes. Excited about his discovery and wanting to share his observation, Sheldon announces emphatically, "If things are red, they sink!"

Often, preschoolers seem to latch onto a faulty reason and insist upon it. They need to go through many illogical thinking processes before they can even begin to make sense of concepts, such as sinking or floating. They must have many experiences with objects so that over time they can assimilate information and organize it to make sense out of what they understand. Eventually, four-year-olds like Sheldon may become aware that some items sink in water, while others float. However, they probably believe that heavy ones sink, and just the light ones float. They usually do not yet understand density.

At snack time, Mrs. Hill's preschoolers are eating avocados. They are overjoyed to see the size of the seed inside. They have been looking at seeds with magnifying glasses at the science table, but nothing looks as big as the avocado seed! After snack, several children ask Mrs. Hill to find information on the Internet so they can learn more about avocados. They print out pictures of the avocado and the seed, then dictate a title, "Our Biggest Seed." During the next few days, some four-year-olds begin to make comparisons about which plants have bigger or smaller seeds, and they design a graph. Over the next few weeks, after the preschoolers decide to plant the seeds to see what

happens, some three-year-olds talk about the growth and changes they are observing. This helps them begin to understand that plants are living things.

Interesting things are happening spontaneously on the playground too. Payton and Kaylee, three-year-olds, have been experimenting over the past week with their shadows. When they are in the sun on the blacktop, they see their shadows. But in the shade under the trees, their shadows disappear. Most three-year-olds, like these girls, begin to realize that light makes shadows. Four-year-olds Felipe and Manish are exploring their shadows also. They hold hands and dance wildly, and their shadows dance too. Four-year-olds are able to think about how to change the size and the shape of their shadows.

Curious and imaginative, investigating scientific principles is a wonderful way for pre-schoolers to expand upon their conceptual understandings of the world around them.

What You Can Do

- **Decorate a science word wall.** Invite your young scientists to contribute some of the words they are learning with their experiments. Ask for their help with organization. They might want to organize the words by broad categories, such as animals and plants, or by themes, such as seeds or magnets. The scientists can draw pictures of the word. So for *gravity*, a child might draw a teddy bear falling off the climbing bars. They can also search for illustrations on the Internet. Encourage children to refer to the words when they write or draw in their journals.

- **Create a collection corner.** Preschoolers love to collect things, from shiny pebbles to tiny toy trucks. Store collections of scientific interest in see-through plastic boxes so children can investigate them independently. You might consider collections of rocks, dried gourds, sea-shells, and so on. Invite children to bring in their own personal collections to share and explore with their friends.

- **Provide engineering opportunities.** Offer materials—such as blocks, ramps, wrapping paper tubes, small balls, and little cars—that provide opportunities to design, test, and solve problems as preschoolers engage in engineering experiments. Give the children several chances over time to explore objects rolling down ramps. Encourage them to make guesses and predictions. Let them change angles and items to roll. What makes things go faster? Slower? Can the ball turn corners? They are learning about physics, gravity, and speed.

- **Go out or invite an expert in.** There are so many places for children to visit to motivate them to want to learn more about various areas of science. You might go to a greenhouse, a nursery, a planetarium, a zoo, a natural history museum, a gem shop, a farm, an aquarium, or a high school robotics fair. Listen to what your children are interested in, and plan a visit.

Or invite a consultant or parent expert to come to school. This makes information gathering more informal and personal. Think about involving an engineer, a veterinarian, a beekeeper, a geologist, a nutritionist, a weather reporter, or a 4H club member. Encourage the preschoolers to develop some questions to ask the expert about things they want to know more about.

- **Plant a garden plot.** Select a space with sun, good soil, and a nearby water source. Invite different expert guests, such as local garden-club members or parents with green thumbs, to help the children get started. Obtain or ask for donations for proper tools—such as shovels, trowels, and watering cans—for the children. Dig up the garden plot. Work with the guest gardener to plant seeds or seedlings. Water when needed. Keep graphs and take digital pictures of plant growth and changes for documentation. Try different types of gardens—maybe for herbs, salads, flowers, or Halloween pumpkins. If you don't have a garden spot outside, you can use a soil-filled grow bag inside.

Other Aspects to Consider—Alerts

- **Resist solving problems.** Don't jump right in. Allow the children to solve their own problems. Because their thinking can be illogical at times, they may not see things the way adults do. Try not to correct them. Mistakes can lead them on a journey with lots of different possibilities. Trial and error challenges their thinking processes. If they become frustrated, you may want to ask questions, such as "What would happen if . . . ?" This type of thinking prompt will get them started problem solving again.

- **Allow time.** Placing time constraints on children's explorations seriously hinders their abilities to work through problems. Frequently, they need many experiences over several weeks before they can identify the problem or concept they wish to investigate. After they have made a prediction, they need time to focus on their experimentations. They may need to go back and rework some ideas.

- **Consider safety issues.** Science can be fun and exciting, but certain materials can be dangerous. For example, it's interesting for children to take apart broken machines, such as a clock, a phone, or a mechanical toy, to see what makes them work; however, you must check for sharp parts. Children should not handle poisonous or toxic plants, such as a poinsettia. Use breakable instruments, such as a prism, with care. Provide nonbreakable magnifying glasses and mirrors. Use a choke tube to measure small items for young three-year-olds or if any children are still mouthing objects. Certain animals, such as turtles, may carry salmonella.

ACTIVITIES FOR PARENTS TO TRY AT HOME

- **Gather research materials.** At the library, take advantage of nonfiction picture books to read with your young child. They have wonderful, realistic pictures of animals and nature as well as factual information to answer your preschooler's many questions. The Internet offers great pictures and printed ideas too. Two marvelous magazines written just for young children are *Ranger Rick Jr.*, which focuses on animal fun, and *National Geographic Little Kids*, which highlights science and nature. Happy reading!

- **Recycle.** Help your child learn to do her part to keep our earth clean. Ask your child to help separate the trash and learn about properties of materials, such as plastic, glass, metal, and paper. Together, you can pick up pieces of trash outdoors—but only items that are safe to handle—and dispose of them. Celebrate Earth Day in April; your child can make posters or necklaces asking others to care for the environment.

- **Help rescue animals.** If possible, you might think about adopting a rescue animal. Your child would learn what a pet needs to live—food and water, just like humans. Shelter and love help keep pets and humans happy and healthy. If you can't adopt, how can you help these animals? Donate pet food, puppy and kitten toys, and clean towels for bedding. You and your child can volunteer to pet kittens or walk puppies. Create colorful yarn pom-poms for collars so dogs look playful.

- **Make a bathtub science lab.** What a great place for children to investigate different science concepts. What floats and what sinks? Try rubber ducks, soap, and a washcloth. Find a way to get a suction cup soap dish to stick to the wall. Why do some shampoo bubbles get bigger when you run the water? Watch water flow as you pour it out of the cup. Why does the water start to get cold? See how the towel absorbs the water when you dry off.

- **Take night walks.** While walking, listen to the night sounds; you might hear an owl or spring peepers. Look up. What do you see in a dark sky? You might see stars, the moon, or an airplane. Every few nights, check the moon. Does it look the same? Make sketches for comparison. If you have a telescope, check out the stars. Look at star patterns in an astronomy book or on an app such as Star Walk on your digital device. Can you find them in the night sky? Talk about why the day is light and night is dark. Why does your child think we sleep at night? What animals are awake at night?

Related Books to Read with Children

Barner, Bob. 1996. *Dem Bones*. San Francisco: Chronicle Books.

Ehlert, Lois. 1988. *Planting a Rainbow*. San Diego: Harcourt Brace Jovanovich.

Frost, Helen, and Rick Lieder. 2012. *Step Gently Out*. Somerville, MA: Candlewick.

Hoban, Tana. 1990. *Shadows and Reflections*. New York: Greenwillow Books.

Marino, Gianna. 2015. *Night Animals*. New York: Viking.

Paul, Miranda. 2015. *Water Is Water*. New York: Roaring Book Press.

Sayre, April Pulley. 2014. *Rah, Rah, Radishes! A Vegetable Chant*. New York: Little Simon.

Walsh, Ellen Stoll. 2010. *Balancing Act*. New York: Beach Lane Books.

9

EXPLORING **THE**
WRITING PROCESS

Handwriting—a complex process of communicating by coordinating the eyes and hands with a pencil grasp to form letters

As preschoolers develop their handwriting skills, you will see exciting progress. Although the children's involvement with learning to write moves through predictable stages of development, the process itself cannot be tied into a definite timetable. The stages are approximate because not all children develop at the same rate or achieve specific milestones at the same time. The preschoolers' skill development will vary because of the level of their fine motor skills and eye-hand coordination, as well as their opportunities to interpret print experiences and practice through writing activities. You are likely to see some of the following behaviors as preschoolers develop their writing skills:

- Creating print-like scribbles, three-year-olds try to imitate some features of adult writing, such as making a shopping list.
- During a mock writing stage, three- to five-year-olds notice that letters seem to be composed of lines and circles.

- Three-year-olds hold a marker between the first two fingers and thumb to write, much like an adult's grip.

- When children are between four and six years old, they tend to learn to write and spell their own names as one of their first words.

- Four- to six-year-olds develop an awareness of environmental print, and they use examples as a reference when they think of ways to construct their own writing systems.

- Four-year-olds are beginning to understand that letters can match sounds.

Now let's consider some scenarios that show how activities in your classroom might support preschoolers' explorations with writing.

In the block center, three-year-old Will concentrates as he picks up a Lego brick carefully between his thumb and forefinger. Next, he places it on top of his submarine. In the art center, four-year-old Zayda is busy creating a fairy princess necklace. She holds a colored wooden bead in one hand while she perfectly threads a pointed string through the hole in the bead. Later, Will puts on a chef's hat at the snack table and uses an egg beater to whip up some yummy banana pudding. Then he pours juice from a small pitcher into his cup. Now he's ready for snack! Meanwhile, Zayda and her friend play at the puzzle table, where they rotate different pieces until they fit in just the right spots. As they get dressed to go outdoors to the playground, Will manipulates the big buttons on his special Mets jacket. Zayda uses her pincer grasp to pull up the zipper on her sweatshirt.

You might wonder what these activities have to do with developing a preschooler's handwriting skills. As Will maneuvers the big buttons through the slit in the fabric of his Mets jacket and Zayda zips up her sweatshirt, they are both using a pincer grasp when they place their thumbs and forefingers together and push or pull items. These movements help to strengthen the small muscles of the hands. As the children grasp small plastic blocks and string beads together, they are not only improving their thinking and fine motor skills, but also learning to develop keen eye-hand coordination. This type of practice is important because by age three many young children are able to hold a pencil in a grasp just like an adult's grip. Activities similar to these allow them to hold marking implements such as chalk, crayons, and a paintbrush in ways that help to develop their predrawing and prewriting skills. While Zayda turns and places puzzle

Cognitive Development of Three- and Four-Year-Olds

pieces and Will manipulates the egg beater and pours juice, they practice hand-rotating skills that they need in order to coordinate their finger muscles and wrist control to maneuver tools for drawing and writing.

In Ms. Lauren's Head Start classroom, the exciting environment is chock-full of activities, materials, and rich visual print conducive to introducing and involving preschoolers in the writing process. Hanging on the wall is a sparkly birthday chart with the children's pictures, names, and birth dates. Another poster shares the colorful book covers of the preschoolers' five favorite books and highlights the written titles. A chart with pictures and writing in English and Spanish shows the steps for proper hand washing. Wonderful, big signs with words and pictures hang over each center and indicate the locations for the children. And a horizontal alphabet chart is posted right at the preschoolers' eye level, available for easy reference.

Jasmine explains to Ms. Lauren that she saw a tornado on TV and it frightened her. With a thick black crayon she draws a dark twisting circular scribble across the top of the paper. After they discuss her drawing, Jasmine begins twirling in circles singing, "A twisting tornado!" At the pretend restaurant, Armando makes linear scribbles on his waiter's pad as he takes orders. In the dramatic play center, Anahita wants to bake cupcakes for her doll. She looks through the booklet of recipes dictated by other children. She decides to add her own recipe. Anahita scribbles a drawing of cupcakes with a pink marker. Then she makes squiggles as she tells her doll about her famous cupcake recipe. Yum!

During this controlled scribbling stage, around three years of age, preschoolers enjoy pretend writing. They move their marking implements like Jasmine's crayon, usually from left to right as they scribble across the paper, often repeating patterns. They may explore circular scribbling or draw squiggles in a linear fashion. With practice, their hand control increases. Sometimes their drawings or pictures tell a story, such as Jasmine's twisting tornado. When experimenting with print-like scribbles, three- to four-year-old children try to imitate some of the features of adult writing, as the waiter Armando did. Between ages three and five, young children tend to create scribble stories, as they fill the page with lots of squiggles. Then, like Anahita telling about her cupcakes, they describe in depth what it says. They are beginning to conceptualize the writing process.

Sitting next to each other at a rectangular table, Head Start children Ruby and Mila are rolling out long pieces of homemade playdough, then breaking off chunks to create mock letters and silly shapes. They place them on word-like strings across the table. At the writing center, Sawyer works independently writing letter-like forms in groups with colored pencils. After writing across the unlined paper, he begins another line and his list progresses down the page. Ms. Ginny, the assistant teacher, has a conference with Sawyer about his writing sample. He has created mock letters with lines and circles, and many of the letters appear reversed or misshapen. Sawyer eagerly explains that this is a list of his favorite superheroes to share with his buddy Keung.

In this mock writing stage, which children usually reach between three and five years of age, preschoolers notice that letters seem to be composed of lines and circles. For example, the girls make mock dough letters by adding several extra lines to an *E* and placing two rolls for an *L* in reverse as they have fun experimenting. Mila makes a string of some fat *O*'s and a few skinny ones. As Sawyer discusses his writing with Ms. Ginny, it is clear that he makes a distinction between drawing and writing as he shares his superhero list with her. At this stage, preschoolers occasionally write for a particular purpose, as Sawyer does with his list. Ms. Ginny notes that he wrote a letter many different ways. In children's letter strings at this stage, normally you don't see separate letters, as you would see with words at a later stage. The writing typically doesn't correspond to sounds or words.

The day before, four-year-old David printed his name at the easel with capital letters. Today, he wants Ms. Lauren to show him how to paint his name like she does with little letters. She creates a large sample for him, talking about the brush strokes as she makes them: "Make a little circle and a little line down for the small *a*." Smiling, David paints his name under Ms. Lauren's example. Pointing, he shows his teacher. "Look, David has two *d*'s—here and here," he says while pointing at the first and last letters. He then paints a picture of himself.

Four-year-old Brielle asks Ms. Ginny to move the birthday chart over to the computer center. At first, Brielle enthusiastically types her own name on the computer. Then she finds a friend's picture on the chart. Together, she and Ms. Ginny talk about the first letter and sound in each child's name. Next, they search for the letter on the keyboard so Brielle can type the letter. She draws a picture with crayons on computer paper of several smiling friends. After printing *FRNS* for *friends*, she tapes both pages together. Jaxon and Liam pack damp sand into large plastic letter molds. When they dump the *N* over, they begin to laugh. They show Ms. Lauren how the *N* on its side can be a *Z*!

Between four and six years of age, young children tend to name and form actual letters in an early phonemic stage. Understandably, one of the first words most children learn to spell is their own name, like David did, as they develop a strong sense of self. They also learn that a name starts with a capital letter and then follows with lowercase ones. They like to label their pictures and note that the beginning sound of their drawing matches the letter, for example, *D* in David. At this stage, children start to understand the *alphabetic principle*, which is that letters make up words and letters represent sounds and then that those letter-sound relationships can help in reading unfamiliar words. This can be observed as Brielle works at the computer and also when she creates the label "FRNS" on her

Cognitive Development of Three- and Four-Year-Olds

picture. At this letter-writing stage, young children enjoy writing friends' and family members' names or words with personal meanings. They have an awareness of environmental print, as evidenced by Brielle's copying the information on the birthday chart. Usually, most letters are written correctly, although some may have reversals. The boys certainly had fun spotting the *N* and *Z* in the sand!

At the Early Learning Center, Mrs. Herbert's four-year-old class went to visit the cookie factory. Back at school, they talk about all of the exciting things they observed. Then Mrs. Herbert uses an experience chart to model authentic writing as the preschoolers dictate the words in a thank-you note to the bakers. Next, they read their words of appreciation for the tasty tour.

The four-year-olds decide to create a book about their cookie factory tour. Each child draws an illustration with magic markers on a construction-paper page. Next, they write their thoughts about their pictures. They use invented or phonetic spelling as they write their word groupings. A few preschoolers will write one letter for each syllable they hear in a word, such as *IC* for *icing*. Others include only letters they think are important, as in writing *HT* for *hot*. Some write long words for large objects, such as *mseeen* for *machine*. When the children are done drawing and writing, Mrs. Herbert binds the pages of the class book so they can read it together at circle time. Then their special written document goes into their library to be read over and over again.

So proud of her ability to bounce two balls, Molly uses chalk to draw a picture of herself. She excitedly writes a whole sentence: *ME Bz 2 Bls*. That is how she communicates her description *Me bouncing two balls*.

This transitional stage of spelling and this invented and phonetic way of writing words frequently occurs between four and seven years of age. As children think of ways to construct their own writing systems, it is important for them to see examples of writing words for practical reasons, such as Mrs. Herbert printing the class thank-you note. This is an extremely exciting stage of writing for young children as they begin to write some real words. They tend to be able to use a mature grip on the writing tool, and the dominant hand is usually quite well developed. At this stage, the use of lowercase letters is becoming more common, as demonstrated by the word *mseeen* for *machine* when the children were writing for the cookie factory book.

The journey from scribbling to creating letters to writing words is empowering for emergent writers. It leads the way to reading, which will only continue to open many more new doors as preschoolers grow and develop.

WHAT YOU CAN DO

- **Introduce multisensory materials.** Offer lots of different ways for preschoolers to practice and create letters: WikkiStix to bend; playdough to manipulate; ink pads with alphabet stamps for printing; trays of salt, sand, or shaving cream to draw fingers through; letter stencils to trace around; a self-erasing magic slate with a writing stylus; a miniature chalkboard to write on with colored chalk; and memo boards with erasable markers. See what else the children can discover, such as writing on the sidewalk with soft rocks.

- **Provide a variety of writing opportunities.** In the dramatic play center, supply paper and markers for writing a shopping list or recipes in the kitchen. The doctor's office needs a prescription pad and an appointment book. The bank could use some checks, and the police officer requires a pad for speeding tickets. The post office can house individual mailboxes created from a beverage box turned on its side. Attach class members' names for delivery of messages. Of course, stationery, envelopes, greeting cards, and box labels would be enticing to emergent writers.

- **Explore different writing surfaces.** Tape butcher paper for a mural to the floor so it won't move while the children work on it. Then invite several children to a party for sharing their writing, at whatever stage they are in. Write single letters on each page of a sticky pad, and then tear them off. Can the writers mix and match letters and create some sticky words? Encourage the preschoolers to take clipboards and paper around the room or outside to sketch and write down their observations.

- **Have children create personal journals.** Entice children to write (whatever their version of writing is) every day in their very own journals. Meet with individuals so you can have conferences about their writing and pertinent illustrations. Talk about similarities in letters and words. Provide an author's chair for those who might like to share their writing with their peers. The writer can read while other children listen and critique the work. Audience members can comment on what they like about the writing.

- **Display writing proudly.** Design an eye-level bulletin board near the writing center. Young children are learning that writing has meaning, so it is important for them to see that their writing is valued and can be shared with others. Encourage the young writers to sign their work. Ask them to help you display writing samples that they feel represent them. Rotate their work to keep the bulletin board fresh and intriguing. Save individual samples so children can observe their progress and the techniques used.

Other Aspects to Consider—Alerts

- **Watch for difficulty with fine motor control.** You may notice that a child seems rather frustrated because he is having a hard time holding or controlling his writing tool. A child's poor motor coordination may be because of dyspraxia, which can cause problems with motor planning and execution. Using modified writing tools that are easier to manipulate might be helpful. For example, children could try thicker pencils or tetrahedron-shaped crayons designed for easier grasping. If these don't help improve the child's fine motor control, the parents may want to consult a pediatrician for diagnostic screening.

- **Check certain general milestones.** If a child between four and five years of age is still holding a crayon in her fist to draw or write or she just randomly scribbles rather than attempting a variety of strokes, this should raise a red flag. Other causes for concern are if the child cannot draw a straight line or circles and is having difficulty remembering how to make various shapes. If any of these continue and modeling doesn't help, you might talk to the parents about referring the child to her doctor, a vision specialist, or a physical therapist.

- **Avoid using workbooks and worksheets.** Preschoolers need to use unlined paper to flex their fine motor skills and express their creativity. They should not need to feel stressed about having to stay on or between the lines as they create their writing. Worksheets are often boring and unrelated to children's interests; they also frequently require a particular answer. It is better for young children to learn letter-sound correspondence as they draw and write from their own ideas and experiences.

Activities for Parents to Try at Home

- **Model authentic writing.** Let your child see how important writing is in your everyday activities. Talk with him as you write shopping lists, birthday cards, checks to pay bills, email messages, fill out forms, and jot down appointments on the calendar. Ask him to help you by labeling his name on his backpack and lunch bag.

- **Create a writing space.** If you have room, provide a small table for writing. If not, use a cardboard box turned upside down. Include a writing basket to hold writing supplies, such as thick pencils and crayons, and an assortment of unlined paper, old greeting cards, index cards, and sticky notes. Laminate a small alphabet chart. To personalize the space, add a small bulletin board to tack up your child's current writing examples to share with the family.

- **Facilitate writing on the go.** When you have to wait at the dentist's office or at a restaurant, have a plastic ziplock bag of writing goodies with you. Collect small pads, colored index cards, colored pencils, and crayons. Add some fun stickers to put on the cards, and see if your child can write some of the letters in the name of the item shown on the sticker. Play a game of drawing or writing the names of things in the room, or create a favorite food menu.

- **Encourage writing outdoors.** Writing doesn't just take place indoors; look at street and traffic signs, check out billboards, and take in storefront signs. Encourage your child to write colorful chalk messages on the sidewalk to neighbors passing by. For writing that turns invisible on windy days, let your child paint letters with water on the sidewalk and buildings. Encourage finger writing in the sandbox. Create interestingly shaped letters with pebble designs.

- **Demonstrate wacky writing.** Partially fill a ziplock bag with paint. Zip it closed. Next, have the child smooth it out for a unique writing surface. Children can write away with their fingers on top of the bag, and then magically erase their manipulations by smoothing the paint out again with their hands. For another fascinating surface, buy a nonbreakable mirror. Offer your child a bar of soft soap as a tricky writing implement. Scribble soapy shapes and letters. Then wash them away and start again!

Related Books to Share with Children

Ahlberg, Allan, and Janet Ahlberg. 2006. *The Jolly Postman, or Other People's Letters.* New York: LB Kids.

Carle, Eric. 2007. *Eric Carle's ABC.* New York: Grosset & Dunlap.

Keats, Ezra Jack. 1998. *A Letter to Amy.* New York: Viking.

Kenney, Sean. 2012. *Amazing ABC: An Alphabet Book of Lego Creations.* New York: Henry Holt.

Martin, Bill Jr., and John Archambault. 2012. *Chicka, Chicka Boom Boom.* New York: Simon & Schuster Books for Young Readers.

Rey, H. A. 1973. *Curious George Learns the Alphabet.* New York: HMH Books for Young Readers.

Williams, Garth. 2015. *Bunnies' ABC.* New York: Golden Books.

10

DEVELOPING EMERGENT READING SKILLS

Reading—making sense from print

As preschoolers interact with print, they develop various capabilities that help prepare them for reading. This is such an exciting time! Although not all children develop at the same rate or achieve specific milestones at the same time, you can expect to see many of the following signs of evolving reading skills:

- While being read to, three-year-olds learn book concepts and mechanics, such as finding the cover on the front where they can locate the title and turning book pages one at a time.
- Three-year-olds are able to sing or recite the alphabet in a rote manner with some prompts.
- Three-year-olds are able to recognize many books by their covers and love to hear certain books read aloud a number of times, particularly in one sitting.
- Four-year-olds know that words are read from left to right in English, as well as top to bottom, and that a book is read from front to back.

- Four-year-olds understand that a book has a beginning, a middle, and an end.
- Four-year-olds know how to recognize words that begin with the same sound, for instance *can* and *cat*.

If we look at some more in-depth examples, we can see how emergent reading skills might show up in your classroom as preschoolers explore their developing cognitive abilities.

Guided by the National Head Start Standards for Emerging Literacy, Mrs. Ettlee and her assistant teacher, Ms. Rashawn, make sure the print-rich experiences in their center are relevant to the children's daily lives. A colorful, large alphabet strip with upper- and lower-case letters and corresponding picture sounds runs along a long wall. A check-in pocket chart with each child's name and photo is right by the door. The menu for breakfast is printed on an easel blackboard. The preschoolers can sort through magazine picture cut-outs of breakfast foods to stick next to the words when they find a match. In the home area, children can play with empty boxes of food labeled in their home languages. A large song chart with the words for one of their favorite songs, "B-I-N-G-O," is displayed in the music area. The technology center has a computer available for the children to type their names and stories, and then print them out to try reading to their friends. The shelves in the art center have storage boxes labeled with materials and appropriate pictures cut from school supply catalogs of such things as pipe cleaners, pom-poms, and colored pencils. A huge bulletin board is labeled with the title "Our Park." After a walk to the city park, the preschoolers paint park pictures and attempt their version of signing their names. A few children dictate little park stories to be read. The block area is decorated with travel posters. Mrs. Ettlee has highlighted architectural features with words to be read, such as *bridge, skyscraper, lighthouse*, and *church*. Outdoors, Ms. Rashawn and a group of boys create road signs so the recognizable environmental print—*stop, one way*, and *school*—can be read by the tricycle and scooter drivers.

Involving more than just decoding words, emergent reading can be embedded in preschoolers' everyday activities throughout their whole day.

Reading activities need to include a large portion of their environment. Emergent reading skills in three- and four-year-olds can be developed through hands-on involvement with and exposure to print-related activities and conversations.

Research indicates that the single most important activity for literacy success and developing skills and understanding is reading aloud to young children. The following examples highlight several interesting classrooms where literature is shared daily.

Ms. Williston is sitting on a big comfortable floor pillow with a book in her hands. Several three-year-olds pull over cozy pillows, and Sybbie sits right on Ms. Williston's lap. They check out the book cover. The teacher points to the words in the title *Eric Carle's ABC* as she reads it. Toula says, "Oh, an ABC book. The alphabet!" Sybbie immediately starts to sing the alphabet song. The others chime right in! Motivated to begin reading the book by author Eric Carle, Sybbie helps turn the pages. This simple book has one letter and one word on each foldable flap page. Excited, the children look at the first picture and identify it, saying the word *ants*. Ms. Williston reads and underlines the *A* with her finger, then repeats the word *ants*. Sybbie turns the page. The three-year-olds say the word *bird*. Bethany's finger touches the *B*. "Hey, my name begins with *B*," she says. "*B* for *Bethany*." "And *bird*," adds Toula. As they read the book together, the preschoolers begin to notice that all the ABC words are animals, such as *F* for *frog*. Knowing in advance that the three-year-olds would love the simple alphabet book, Ms. Williston has already prepared a follow-up. She sets out a few large plastic letters on the manipulatives table. She wants to see if the children can match the plastic letters with the first few letters on the full-page unfolded flap spread open on the table.

Three-year-olds love to be read to, especially in a cozy atmosphere. While being read to, they learn about various book concepts, such as finding the cover on the front of the book. Then they are able to locate the title on the front cover. As Toula discovered, they can use the cover to predict what the story is about. Young children practice by turning the pages one at a time, as Sybbie did. The children in Ms. Williston's class were excited about the ABCs book and were happy to sing the alphabet song together. At this age, they are able to recite the alphabet in a rote manner with some prompting. Three-year-olds not only enjoy listening to a story, but they also like to talk about the book; for example, the preschoolers are excited to find that all of the words represent types of animals. The three-year-olds discover that they can identify and match some letters as well as make a few letter-sound matches. A three-year-old is frequently able to match the first letter in her name with that letter in print, as evidenced by Bethany's discovery.

In another classroom, Mrs. Grossman's four-year-old boys are having a great time teasing each other for fun, as four-year-old boys tend to like to do. Adam says, "Hey Bobby-wobby. Give me that long log." Bobby retorts, "OK, Adam-badam. I'll shoot it over to you." Mrs. Grossman picks up on the boys' interest in playing with silly rhyming words. She knows just the rhyming book to read with the group, *Llama Llama Red Pajama* by Anna Dewdney. After the preschoolers identify the character on the book cover as a silly-looking llama and say the words in the title, emphasizing the sounds of the rhyming words *llama* and *pajama*, they have a good laugh. They watch Mrs. Grossman intently as she moves her finger under the words from left to right and down the page. It's easy for the children to catch on to the four-line rhymes. They enjoy acting out their favorite one, "Baby Llama stomps and pouts. Baby Llama jumps and shouts." At the end, Mama Llama reassures her little one, who then "snuggles pillows soft and deep. Baby llama goes to sleep." Teá enthusiastically adds, "Guess what? Our president's name, Obama, rhymes with llama." The preschoolers think that her discovery is very cool. Adam holds the book so the four-year-olds can find some of the rhymes, while Mrs. Grossman writes them in pairs on a chart. Teá notices that the sound of *L* in *Llama* is like a little song, "lah-lah."

Most four-year-olds truly enjoy the sounds of rhyming words, which is probably why they delight in hearing their parents and teachers read nursery rhymes to them. Many are able to recognize words that end alike or rhyme, such as *cat*, *hat*, and *rat*. Four-year-olds, like Adam, tend to know the mechanics and conventions of reading. For example, they know how to hold and look at a book right side up, that words are read from left to right in English and top to bottom on the page, and that the book is read from front to back. Some four-year-olds, like Teá, are able to match certain letters with their sounds, such as the *L* with /lah/.

In Mrs. B's big rocking chair, Drew is reading a book to his pretend class. He has heard this special book, which is filled with simple, predictable lines, many times. Four-year-old Drew is able to retell or attempt to read the story independently to his make-believe group with the help of picture prompts and the predictable text, *It Looked Like Spilt Milk* by Charles Shaw. This is a wonderful, classic concept book that encourages memory reading. It helps a young child recite because it uses similar phrasing in a pattern: "Sometimes it looked like a Rabbit. But it wasn't a Rabbit." Drew loves being able to appear to read to his little group because he has memorized language patterns and repeated refrains.

Other preschoolers ask Mrs. B to let them help her read another favorite predictable book, *Brown Bear, Brown Bear, What Do You See?* by Bill Martin Jr. They help her read the repeating pattern, "Brown Bear, Brown Bear, What do you see? I see a red bird looking at me. Red Bird, Red Bird, What do you see?" and so on. The children have created animal puppets out of paper plates, and they raise them when the appropriate picture prompts appear. It is obvious that they are having a delightful time actively responding to the predictable text and colorful pictures. Now, Mrs. B invites the three- and four-year-olds to design a story circle with her. On the Internet, they find colored illustrations of the animals in the book. After cutting them out and labeling them, they talk about the sequence in the story where each character belongs. Using a giant mural paper circle, the preschoolers glue the animals sequentially, clock style, as they retell the story. Now the Brown Bear story circle is available in the beginning, the middle, and the end for the developing readers to share with each other.

Three-year-olds are often able to request stories by name and enjoy exploring books independently as emergent readers. Three-year-olds, like the ones in Mrs. B's class, truly enjoy hearing certain stories read aloud a number of times, sometimes more than once in one session. With more experience handling books and being read to, three-year-olds are able to recognize numerous books by their covers and are excited to tell about the stories inside the books. Preschoolers like Drew have fun pretending to read. They are clearly able to make a distinction between pictures and print. As evidenced by the children in Mrs. B's class, using picture clues along with predictable text enables preschoolers to follow a story sequence. They are aware of the parts of the story: beginning, middle, and end. Four-year-olds tend to be comfortable asking questions and making comments about books. This indicates that they understand what is read to them.

In a different preschool, Mr. Dirvin is taking his class to visit a cookie factory where one child's dad works. They frequently eat cookies from Werner's dad for snack, so they are excited about the trip. When they return with their heads filled with delicious smells, the children want to bake cookies. Mr. Dirvin asks if they would like to read a story with a recipe for a special cookie. The preschoolers laugh when he surprises them with *The*

Gingerbread Man. They immediately respond to the predictable, cumulative patterns in the text: "Run, run as fast as you can. You can't catch me, I'm the gingerbread man!" They say them along with Mr. Dirvin as he reads the lines. They are thrilled to find the little old woman's printed recipe. Ginny comments, "My grandmother bakes cookies. She uses a recipe too." As they continue reading with great enthusiasm, the attentive children comment on the different characters. They anticipate what the sly fox will do. During this whole-group shared reading, the preschoolers respond to Mr. Dirvin's prompts and questions, such as "How would you help the gingerbread man?" After the class decides to put him in a kayak, Ryder teases and announces, "I'd eat him!" When the teacher uses the white board to write the first few lines, they strive to read it together. Mr. Dirvin asks what they see and hear. They quickly point out the rhymes, such as *can* and *man*. They see and hear three words that begin with the letter *C*—*can*, *can't*, and *catch*. MaryJo shows the spaces between words.

Now the children are really ready to follow the recipe that Mr. Dirvin has reprinted in an easier-to-read rebus form. They use cookie cutters to cut out their own gingerbread men and bake them—just like in the book. While waiting for them to bake and then cool, they have a wonderful time taking turns dramatizing this deliciously classic folk tale. Yum!

Most three-year-olds are beginning to understand that some books contain pretend stories, such as *The Gingerbread Man*, and others give real information, such as an alphabet book. Three-year-olds also tend to realize that letters are used to make words, for example, *run* or *Ginny*. Four-year-olds usually have learned that words in a book communicate meaning, such as *old* before the word *woman*. They also know how to recognize words that begin with the same sound, such as *can*, *can't*, and *catch*. It is fun for them to act out the plots in stories. They have a great interest in characters, such as the fox, and their roles in a book.

Using books as a springboard to enhance young children's potential to become lifelong readers is certainly an important way to involve them in a continuously literacy-rich environment.

What You Can Do

■ **Create an inviting classroom library.** Include a variety of types of publications, such as poetry, wordless books, special favorites, fairy tales, informational books, songs, copies of the preschoolers' original stories, and children's magazines. Provide about six books per child. Depending on your preschoolers' interests and the projects they are involved in, rotate a portion of your books every three weeks or so. Place themed books in various centers for reference. For example, you might stock books about heavy construction equipment in the block center. Put some books low on a rack with the covers facing out for easy selection. Make the space cozy with a soft chair or a big floor pillow for one-on-one readings with you or small-group interactive readings with friends. On the wall, add colorful book posters or original story drawings by your children.

- **Explore wordless books.** With these books, the story is imparted through the illustrations. Wordless stories encourage the reader to share what is happening with his own words. Two children may actually create different stories from reading the pictures. Together, talk your way through the pages and discuss the details you see in the pictures. Now, read the story and encourage the children to use interesting sound effects, such as "woof-woof, growl," and expressive voices for the characters. Ask readers questions to enhance details and add interesting words. For fun, I like to write their words on sticky notes, which I attach to each page so we can keep sharing ideas, reading the story, and changing their versions. Wordless books also can support vocabulary development in dual language learners.

- **Show that not all print tells a story.** Children need to be exposed to a variety of types of environmental print so they can learn that print has various uses and meanings. In the dra-

matic play center, provide children's cookbooks, store coupons, a pad for to-do lists, and lots of junk mail to open and read. In the restaurant area, offer menus, posters showing the specials of the day, a waiter's pad, and bills for the meals. While out on a walk, take pictures of signs, such as a stop sign, or

those designating a park, a bank, a post office, or parking. Print them out to make a collection of signs the children can read. See if the preschoolers can look at the pictures on packaging and labeling and sound out the words—for example, on game boxes or food containers. Turn the pages together to look at the pictures and words in reference materials, such as in *My First Dictionary* by Susan A. Miller.

- **Communicate through dictation.** Writing down children's words while they say them and then reading their thoughts helps them see a relationship between spoken words and print. Record their words as they investigate scientific problems, so they can share their exciting findings with others. Often children enjoy dictating a story about their artwork. A group of preschoolers might like to create pictures about something of interest, such as engineering an airport out of blocks or visiting the pumpkin patch. After writing down their dictation, the children can help you bind the pages into a book to read and share in their library.

- **Play with rhymes and other sounds of language.** Research shows the importance of playing with rhymes and chants as a way of developing a child's phonetic awareness. Read a nursery rhyme and pause to have the preschoolers fill in the rhyming word. For example, you might read "Jack and Jill went up the…" and let them fill in the word. Listen and clap on the rhyming patterns in chants and jump-rope rhymes. For example, chant, "Teddy bear, Teddy bear jump so high. Teddy bear, Teddy bear touch the sky." Make a game of word families. On a strip of paper print *man*. Staple a half strip on top so only the ending *-an* shows. Add a letter on the overlay to create another word in the family (*p* + *an* = *pan*). Build more rhymes—such as *can* and *fan*—with letters on top. This creates a little rhyming-family flip booklet.

OTHER ASPECTS TO CONSIDER—ALERTS

- **Don't make workbooks a part of your program.** Because workbooks usually are not relevant to young children's interests, they are not really appropriate for preschoolers. They normally require children to give a correct answer, which can be quite stressful. They often require preschoolers to be passive when following directions instead of being critical or creative thinkers. Instead, encourage children to play hands-on letter and sound games and explore the sounds of words while reading books together.

- **Do not incorporate a push-down formal reading curriculum.** With high-stakes testing in elementary school, educators keep trying to move the teaching of reading concepts down into kindergarten and preschool. Instead, young children thrive on a print-rich environment with conversations that are meaningful to them. It is important for preschoolers to have lots of time to explore books, paint, and participate in dramatic play activities without feeling pressured.

- **Observe for hints of language delays.** Usually, language difficulties first appear with spoken language. A preschooler may mispronounce words and use baby talk. She may not show interest in rhymes and may have difficulty reciting nursery rhymes. The child might have difficulty learning the letters in her name or remembering letter names. She might need to be referred to her pediatrician, who might suggest a professional therapist to work with the child and evaluate her language skills.

ACTIVITIES FOR PARENTS TO TRY AT HOME

- **Surround your emergent reader with books.** Take your child to the public library to choose books for you to read together. Have him try signing his library card. Libraries and book stores have wonderful story hours for children on a regular basis. If you live in a rural area, you might be able to visit a bookmobile. The librarian might be able to order books for your child based on his interest. Flea markets and garage sales are inexpensive and fun places to purchase books for your child's personal library.

- **Create a new ending.** Just because the story ends in the book you are reading doesn't mean that you and your child can't continue the story. Use your imaginations to tell, write down, and then read your new ending. For example, what if Goldilocks brought cookies back to share with the bears to apologize? Could they become friends? Could they go on a picnic together? Keep adding to the story!

- **Use your computer, smartphone, or tablet.** Help your child build her reading skills using technology devices. There are numerous stories that your child can have read to her—such as *The Cat in the Hat* by Dr. Seuss and *The Monster at the End of This Book* by Jon Stone—using a smartphone or computer. Word and letter games are available on the PBS Kids website (http://pbskids.org/games/). Leapfrog offers letter and word identification activities. Many apps for smartphones or computers let you design customized personal storybooks to zero in on your child's special interest.

- ■ **Explore alphabet letter fun.** Young children are interested in exploring the letters of the alphabet through broad and focused activities. Your child may enjoy using her fingers as a writing instrument in sand, kosher salt, or nonmenthol shaving cream. She can form letter shapes with pipe cleaners, thick yarn chunks, or rolled playdough. Play a game of matching upper- and lowercase letters printed on index cards. Try putting together alphabet puzzles. Your child also might like tracing around the thick letters from the puzzle. Try a concentration game by turning over alphabet letter cards and looking for matches.

- ■ **Create letter collages.** Have available a variety of print materials, such as magazines, newspapers, junk mail, and packaging, along with scissors, glue sticks, construction paper, and crayons. Encourage your child to pick a letter—maybe one that's in his name. Let him find and cut out as many of the selected letters as possible. Glue them on the paper. If he can, encourage him to print the letter with the crayon. Draw or cut out pictures of things that begin like the sound of the letter, such as *ball* and *boat* for the letter *B*. Add to the letter page from time to time or connect the pages to make a child-created letter book.

RELATED BOOKS TO READ WITH CHILDREN

ABC Books

Carle, Eric. 2007. *Eric Carle's ABC*. New York: Grosset and Dunlap.

Carter, David A. 2006. *Alpha Bugs: A Pop-Up Alphabet*. New York: Little Simon.

Dr. Seuss. 1991. *Dr. Seuss's ABC: An Amazing Alphabet Book!* New York: Random House.

Ehlert, Lois. 1989. *Eating the Alphabet: Fruits and Vegetables from A to Z*. Boston: Houghton Mifflin Harcourt.

Kirk, David. 1998. *Miss Spider's ABC*. New York: Scholastic.

Metropolitan Museum of Art. 2002. *Museum ABC*. Boston: Little, Brown.

Rhyming Books

Ahlberg, Janet, and Allan Ahlberg. 1999. *Each Peach Pear Plum*. New York: Viking.

Asim, Jabari, and LeUyen Pham. 2006. *Whose Toes Are Those?* New York: Little, Brown.

Degan, Bruce. 2014. *Jamberry*. New York: HarperCollins.

Dewdney, Anna. 2005. *Llama Llama Red Pajama*. New York: Viking.

Donaldson, Julia. 2006. *The Gruffalo*. New York: Puffin Books.

Parragon. 2012. *The Gingerbread Man*. Bath, UK: Parragon.

Shaw, Nancy. 1996. *Sheep in a Jeep*. Boston: Houghton Mifflin.

Predictable Books

Brown, Margaret Wise. 2006. *The Runaway Bunny*. New York: HarperCollins.

Carle, Eric. 2001. *Today Is Monday*. New York: Philomel Books.

Emberley, Barbara, and Ed Emberley. 1987. *Drummer Hoff*. New York: Simon and Schuster Books for Young Readers.

Krauss, Ruth. 2004. *The Carrot Seed 60th Anniversary Edition*. New York: HarperCollins.

Martin, Bill Jr. 1996. *Brown Bear, Brown Bear, What Do You See?* New York: Henry Holt.

Numeroff, Laura Joffe. 2015. *If You Give a Mouse a Cookie*. New York: HarperCollins.

Shaw, Charles G. 2008. *It Looked Like Spilt Milk*. New York: HarperCollins.

Wordless Picture Books

Briggs, Raymond. 1978. *The Snowman*. New York: Random House Books for Young Children.

dePaola, Tomie. 1978. *Pancakes for Breakfast*. New York: Harcourt Brace Jovanovich.

Mayer, Mercer. 2003. *A Boy, a Dog, and a Frog*. New York: Dial Books for Young Readers.

Rathmann, Peggy. 1996. *Good Night Gorilla*. New York: Putnam.

Savage, Stephen. 2011. *Where's Walrus?* New York: Scholastic.

11

MILESTONES
IN COGNITIVE
DEVELOPMENT

Now that you have explored the cognitive skills highlighted in this book and the classroom examples provided, you might want to review and reflect on the important milestones children tend to reach in their preschool years. Although these characteristics are typical of many three- and four-year-olds, they are not necessarily true of all preschoolers, nor do they appear at the same times with each child. Recognizing common challenges and successes can help you better prepare for supporting the cognitive development of three- and four-year-olds and celebrate their amazing growth.

Skills	Three-Year-Olds	Four-Year-Olds
Magical thinking	• They use their magical thinking when they really hope that something will happen. • They may illogically attribute the causes of common occurrences.	• They are sometimes confused about whether their thoughts are real or make-believe. • When they use their magical thinking, the causes and effects of events are not always objectively determined.
Sense of curiosity	• Although curious, they often observe others' investigations from a safe distance until they feel comfortable exploring too. • They express curiosity about things that are related to themselves, their bodies, and their families.	• They show their confidence by jumping right in to explore and experiment based on their curiosity. • When curious, they find it helpful to clarify their thinking by looking at items' similarities or differences to assist them in creating a meaningful classification.
Time concepts	• Sometimes, they confuse past and future terms. For instance, a child might say, "I am not going to the park with Anthony yesterday." • They enjoy using lots of words relating to clocks (such as "It is one o'clock"), even though they are not able to read abstract time-telling devices such as analog clocks.	• They understand and comfortably use words for the past, present, and future. • They have the ability to order events sequentially, which leads to the children's understanding of time intervals.
Spatial awareness	• They explore the concept of spatial awareness as they arrange and rearrange items and observe their positions relative to one another. • They express personal knowledge of location and spatial awareness, such as when they name their street.	• They identify prominent landmarks to help pinpoint the location of items. • They learn to create mental pictures to refer to while drawing on a map.
Problem solving	• While relying on their senses instead of reasoning, they frequently solve problems by using a trial-and-error process. • At times, they focus on just one solution, sure that it is the only answer, even when it doesn't work.	• More able to look at ideas from the viewpoint of others, they like solving problems and working cooperatively. • When an item is not available, they use their imaginations and thinking skills to find a creative substitute.

(Continued on next page)

(continued from previous page)

Skills	Three-Year-Olds	Four-Year-Olds
Creativity	• Frequently, their first representational artwork is a person, usually with a big circle head and two lines for legs or a body, rather tadpole-like. • They may name their artwork, which indicates that they are thinking about the mental pictures they have created.	• They may draw or paint several representations randomly on a piece of paper so that they appear to spatially float on the page. • They love to use colors, but they are not overly concerned if their color choices are not appropriate representations (such as blue apples).
Mathematical thinking	• They learn that even when objects are classified together, they can represent different degrees (such as size or brightness) when seriated. • They can identify the basic sequence of a pattern and then extend the pattern.	• Most can count to ten. They understand *cardinality*, when the last number in a counting sequence is the quantity. • They can use nonstandardized measuring units, such as pencils or footsteps, to reproduce length or width.
Investigating science	• Experimentation is a primary method of learning, so they will try various ideas until they find a successful one. • They need many experiences with objects so that over time they can assimilate information and organize it to make sense of what they understand.	• They enjoy experimenting with different materials as they engage in cooperatively planned investigations. • They find it helpful to record information to organize their ideas and may contribute to adult-created charts.
Writing process	• They are able to make a distinction between writing and drawing. • As they make scribbles across a paper in a line, they create pretend writing.	• Although they may name and write letters that are recognizable, they frequently reverse them. • They often use invented or phonetic spelling as they write words by grouping letters together.
Reading skills	• They can identify and match some letters as well as make a few letter-sound matches, such as the first letter in a child's name. • They are beginning to understand that some stories are pretend and others give real information.	• They are able to recognize words that end alike and rhyme. • They are able to memory read predictable books because they have memorized language patterns and repeated refrains.

Cognitive Development of Three- and Four-Year-Olds

INDEX

defined, 36
and fear, 43
milestones for, 93
precautions, 43
and science investigation skills,
    66–67
typical behaviors, 36–41

R

reading, defined, 81
reading aloud, 83
reading skills
    activities for, 86–88, 89–90
    and body awareness, 34
    children's books related to, 90–91
    milestones for, 94
    precautions, 88–89
    typical behaviors, 81–86
rhyming words, 84, 88
rote counting, 57
routines, 23, 26
    See also time concepts

S

Santa Claus, 10
science, defined, 63
science investigation skills
    activities for, 69–70, 71–72
    children's books related to, 72
    milestones for, 94
    precautions, 70–71
    and problem solving, 66–67
    typical behaviors, 63–69
seriation, 55–56
social boundaries, 34
spatial awareness
    activities for, 33, 34–35
    and blocks, 30
    children's books related to, 35
    and computer games, 60

defined, 28
milestones for, 93
precautions, 34
professional help for, 34
typical behaviors, 28
spatial visualization, 30

T

time, defined, 21
time concepts
    activities for, 25, 26–27
    children's books related to, 27
    milestones for, 93
    precautions, 25–26
    and routines, 23, 26
    typical behaviors, 21–24
transitions, 25

W

workbooks, 79, 88
worksheets, 60, 79
writing process
    activities for, 78–80
    and alphabetic principle, 76
    children's books related to, 80
    and fine motor skills, 74–75
    milestones for, 94
    precautions, 79
    professional help for, 79
    typical behaviors, 73–78

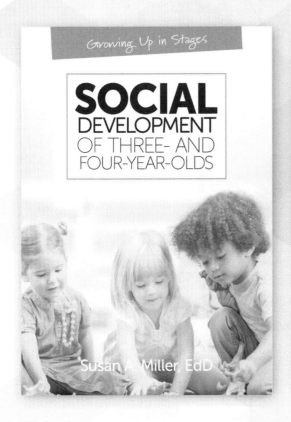
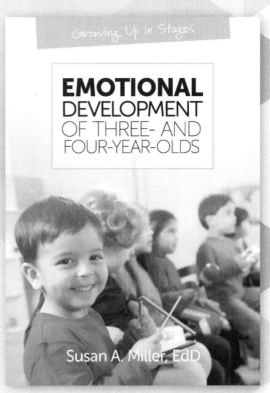